WOMEN BREAKING FREE

Conquer Control Issues, Overcome Perfectionism, Reduce Anxiety, Achieve Work-Life Balance, and Find Inner Peace for Emotional Well-Being

EVE MEADOWS

© Copyright Eve Meadows 2024 - All rights reserved.

The content within this book may not be reproduced, duplicated or transmitted without direct written permission from the author or the publisher.

Under no circumstances will any blame or legal responsibility be held against the publisher or author for any damages, reparation, or monetary loss due to the information contained within this book. Either directly or indirectly. You are responsible for your own choices, actions, and results.

Legal Notice:

This book is copyright-protected and only for personal use. You cannot amend, distribute, sell, use, quote, or paraphrase any part of the content without the consent of the author or publisher.

Disclaimer Notice:

Please note that the information in this document is for educational and entertainment purposes only. All effort has been expended to present accurate, up-to-date, reliable, and complete information. No warranties of any kind are declared or implied. Readers acknowledge that the author does not render legal, financial, medical, or professional advice. The content within this book has been derived from various sources. Please consult a licensed professional before attempting any techniques outlined in this book.

By reading this document, the reader agrees that the author is under no circumstances responsible for any direct or indirect losses incurred from using the information contained within this document, including, but not limited to, errors, omissions, or inaccuracies.

Contents

Introduction ... 7

1. UNDERSTANDING CONTROL BEHAVIORS ... 11
Recognizing the Signs of Control ... 11
The Psychology Behind Control ... 12
How Control Manifests in Daily Life ... 14
The Impact of Control on Mental Health ... 15
How Control Affects Relationships ... 17
Self-Assessment: Are You a Control Freak? ... 19

2. PRACTICAL TOOLS FOR IMMEDIATE CHANGE ... 23
Mindfulness Techniques to Calm the Mind ... 23
Deep-Breathing Exercises for Instant Stress Relief ... 25
Time-Management Tips for a Balanced Life ... 26
Creating Daily Routines for Flexibility ... 28
Setting Realistic Expectations ... 29
Quick Wins: Small Changes with Big Impact ... 31

3. ENHANCING MENTAL HEALTH AND WELL-BEING ... 33
Cognitive-Behavioral Techniques for Anxiety ... 33
Stress-Reduction Methods You Can Start Today ... 35
The Importance of Sleep and Rest ... 37
Nutrition and Its Impact on Mental Health ... 38
Exercise as a Tool for Emotional Balance ... 40
Incorporating Meditation into Your Daily Routine ... 41

4. DEEP SELF-REFLECTION AND AWARENESS ... 45
Reflective Questions to Uncover Hidden Anxieties ... 47
Understanding Your Triggers ... 49
The Role of Past Experiences ... 50

Identifying Fear-Based Thoughts 52
Building Self-Awareness Through Reflection 53

5. IMPROVING RELATIONSHIP DYNAMICS 57
Effective Communication Skills 57
Building Trust with Your Partner 59
Navigating Conflicts Without Control 60
The Power of Active Listening 62
Setting Healthy Boundaries 64
Role-Playing Scenarios for Real-Life Practice 65

6. BALANCING PROFESSIONAL AND PERSONAL LIFE 69
Productivity Hacks for Busy Women 69
Delegation Techniques for the Workplace 71
Reducing Workplace Stress 73
Creating a Work-Life Balance Plan 74
Managing Perfectionism at Work 75
Relaxation Methods for Busy Schedules 77

7. MANAGING TECHNOLOGY AND DIGITAL DISTRACTIONS 79
Impact of Technology on Control Behaviors 79
Strategies for Healthy Technology Use 82
Balancing Technology and Real-Life Interactions 85

8. PARENTING WITHOUT CONTROL 89
Setting Healthy Boundaries with Children 89
Encouraging Independence in Kids 91
Positive Reinforcement Techniques 93
Creating a Nurturing Home Environment 94
Handling Parenting Stress 96
Building Trust with Your Children 97

9. NAVIGATING SOCIETAL AND CULTURAL PRESSURES 101
Breaking Free from Traditional Roles 101
Finding Your Path 103
Handling Societal Expectations 104
Embracing Your Authentic Self 106

Stories of Women Who Overcame Control Issues	108
Strategies for Long-Term Change	109
10. BUILDING A SUPPORT NETWORK	113
Importance of a Support Network	113
Finding and Cultivating Support	116
Maintaining Healthy Relationships	118
Success Stories	120
11. EMBRACING FLEXIBILITY AND ADAPTABILITY	125
Understanding Flexibility	125
Developing Adaptability Skills	128
Real-Life Application	131
12. CREATING A PERSONAL ACTION PLAN	135
Developing an Action Plan	135
Setting Milestones and Rewards	139
Maintaining Motivation	142
Conclusion	145
References	149
Women Breaking Free	153

Introduction

I remember the moment like it was yesterday. I was standing in my kitchen, frantically organizing the cabinets while simultaneously planning the week's meals in my head. The kids were squabbling in the background, my phone buzzing with work emails, and my partner asked me where his clean socks were. I snapped. The pressure of managing every detail, of controlling every outcome, was overwhelming, and I broke down in tears. Sound familiar?

You might be reading this and nodding your head. Maybe you've had moments of feeling like you're holding the world together with duct tape and sheer willpower. If you're a woman juggling multiple roles —professional, partner, mother, friend—you know all too well the stress of trying to control everything. This constant need to manage all aspects of life often leads to anxiety, strained relationships, and a sense of burnout that's hard to shake.

So, what does it mean to be a control freak? It's not a term I use lightly. Being a control freak involves a persistent need to ensure everything around you goes according to plan. It's micromanaging at work because you believe that no one else can do the job as well as you can. It's organizing every family outing down to the minute, fearing that any deviation will lead to chaos. It's the anxiety that bubbles up when things don't go as expected and the frustration that comes from trying to manage outcomes beyond your control.

Control issues are more widespread than you might think. According to various studies, many women feel overwhelmed by the need to control their environments. This behavior is often driven by societal pressures to be perfect in every role we play. The impact on mental health is significant, leading to increased stress, anxiety, and depression. Relationships also suffer, as the need for control can create tension and conflict with loved ones.

I've been there. I've struggled with control issues for years. My wake-up call came when I realized my need to control everything drove a wedge between me and the people I cared about most. I was constantly stressed, racing with to-do lists and contingency plans. I knew something had to change. My journey towards letting go of control wasn't easy, but it was transformative. I learned to embrace uncertainty, to trust others, and to find peace in the present moment. This book reflects that journey and the lessons I've learned.

My vision for this book is simple yet powerful: to empower you to let go of control and embrace a life of balance, peace, and fulfillment. We'll explore practical tools, self-reflection exercises, and holistic strategies to help you manage anxiety, improve relationships, and thrive personally and professionally. This isn't about perfection; it's about progress and growth.

The book is structured to guide you through this transformative process step by step. We'll start by understanding the roots of control issues and how they manifest in your daily life. Then, we'll dive into strategies for enhancing self-awareness and developing healthier thought patterns. You'll find practical advice on managing stress, setting boundaries, and nurturing your emotional well-being. Each chapter ends with reflection exercises to help you apply your learning.

Who is this book for? It's for women like you who are seeking personal growth and balance. It's for those in relationships wanting to improve dynamics and individuals struggling with anxiety and control issues. It's for professional women, parents, and anyone navigating the complex web of societal and cultural expectations. If you're ready to break free from the constraints of control and perfectionism, this book is for you.

I want you to know that this journey won't be perfect, and that's okay. The tone of this book is supportive, empathetic, and informal. I'm here with you every step of the way, offering guidance and encouragement. The advice is easy to follow, with actionable steps and relatable examples to help you make meaningful changes in your life.

Self-awareness is the key to overcoming control issues. By understanding the root causes of your behaviors, you can begin to make conscious choices that lead to healthier, more fulfilling relationships and a more balanced life. This book will guide you through that process, helping you to see yourself and your actions more clearly.

I promise you that transformation is possible. Following this book's guidance, you'll learn to manage anxiety, improve relationships, and thrive personally and professionally. You deserve a life that isn't dictated by the need to control everything. You deserve peace, balance, and fulfillment. Let's take this journey together.

Welcome to a new chapter in your life.

ONE

Understanding Control Behaviors

I once had a friend who would meticulously plan every detail of our weekend getaways. From the exact route we'd take to the type of snacks we'd have, she left no stone unturned. While her organization skills were impressive, they often left little room for spontaneity or relaxation. While seemingly harmless, this need to control every aspect of our trips was a manifestation of deeper control issues. You're not alone if you've ever been in a similar situation. Many of us struggle with the need to control our environments and the people in them, often without even realizing it.

Recognizing the Signs of Control

Control behaviors can be overt and subtle, but they all share a common thread: the need to manage and influence outcomes. Micromanaging tasks are a classic example. You might feel compelled to oversee every detail of a project at work, believing that no one else can execute it to your standards. Insisting on specific ways of doing things, whether it's the laundry or how the dishwasher is loaded, also falls under this umbrella. You may find it difficult to delegate responsibilities, worrying that others won't meet your expectations. This leads to excessive checking and reassurances, constantly verifying that tasks are done "correctly."

Common behaviors signaling a tendency towards control include interrupting others to assert your opinions and becoming anxious when plans change. You might also find yourself constantly correcting others, whether it's your partner's way of folding clothes or your colleague's approach to a task. While seemingly minor, these actions can indicate a deeper issue with control.

Consider these relatable scenarios: A mother meticulously correcting her child's homework, not allowing any room for mistakes, or a manager redoing employee tasks, believing her way is the only right way. These situations create stress and stifle creativity and growth in those around you.

The emotional drivers behind control behaviors are often rooted in fear and anxiety. Fear of failure can make you feel that controlling every aspect of your life will prevent mistakes. Anxiety about the unknown can lead you to over-plan and over-manage, seeking comfort in predictability.

Understanding these signs and emotional drivers is the first step in recognizing and addressing control behaviors. By becoming aware of these tendencies, you can make conscious choices to let go of control, fostering a more balanced and fulfilling life.

The Psychology Behind Control

Understanding the psychology behind control behaviors can be enlightening. Cognitive-behavioral theories offer insights into how our thoughts influence our actions. Cognitive distortions, or faulty thinking patterns, can lead us to believe control is the only way to prevent failure. For instance, black-and-white thinking can make us see situations as perfect or disastrous, pushing us to control every detail to avoid perceived catastrophes. Similarly, overgeneralization can lead us to apply one negative experience to all future situations, reinforcing the need for control.

Attachment theory also plays a significant role in understanding control behaviors. Insecure attachment styles, often developed in childhood, can lead to a heightened need for control in adulthood. If you experienced overprotective parenting, you might have learned that the world is dangerous and controlling every aspect of your environment is the only way to navigate it. Childhood trauma, such as neglect or abuse, can further exacerbate these feelings, making you feel that control is necessary for safety and stability.

Personality traits are another critical factor. Perfectionism, characterized by setting unrealistically high standards, is often linked to control behaviors. Perfectionists may fear making mistakes and feel compelled to control every detail to ensure everything meets their exacting standards. High conscientiousness, the desire for order, structure, and dependability, can also contribute to control behaviors. While these traits can be strengths, they can lead to stress and anxiety when taken to extremes.

Societal and cultural factors cannot be ignored. Societal pressure to succeed, particularly for women, can drive control behaviors. We are often expected to excel in multiple roles—career, family, social life—leading us to believe that control is the only way to meet these expectations. Cultural norms around gender roles also play a part. Traditional expectations that women should manage the household, care for children, and support partners can create an overwhelming sense of responsibility, further fueling the need for control.

Understanding these psychological underpinnings helps us see that control behaviors are not merely quirks but deeply rooted responses to various influences. Recognizing the impact of cognitive distortions, attachment styles, personality traits, and societal pressures allows us to approach the issue with empathy and self-awareness. By exploring these factors, we can unravel the complex web that drives our need for control and take the first steps toward a more balanced and fulfilling life.

How Control Manifests in Daily Life

Control behaviors often seep into the fabric of our daily routines, shaping how we organize and manage our lives. Planning and organizing routines can feel like a lifeline in the chaotic responsibilities swirl. You might find comfort in mapping out every minute of your day, from when you wake up to when you go to bed. This meticulous planning can provide a sense of control and predictability, but it can also become a rigid framework that leaves little room for spontaneity or flexibility. When every aspect of your day is scheduled to the last second, any unexpected event can throw you into a tailspin of anxiety and frustration.

Controlling household chores is another common manifestation. You may need to oversee every task, ensuring everything is done "your way." This could mean dictating how the laundry is folded, how the dishwasher is loaded, or even how the groceries are organized in the pantry. While it's natural to have preferences, insisting on specific ways of doing things can create a tense atmosphere at home. This behavior can also lead to resentment from family members who feel micromanaged and undervalued, straining relationships and creating unnecessary stress.

In professional settings, control behaviors can be both a blessing and a curse. Micromanaging team projects stems from a desire to ensure high-quality outcomes, but it can stifle creativity and autonomy among team members. When you're constantly checking in on every detail, it sends a message that you don't trust others to do their jobs effectively. This can lead to a toxic work environment where colleagues feel demotivated and disengaged. Reluctance to delegate tasks is another hallmark of control in the workplace. By taking on too much yourself, you not only overwhelm your workload but also deny others the opportunity to grow and contribute.

Control behaviors also permeate personal relationships, often in subtle ways. You might find yourself dictating social plans, insisting on specific activities, venues, or schedules. This can make your friends or partner feel like their preferences don't matter, leading to a sense of imbalance in the relationship. Monitoring your partner's actions, whether it's through constant check-ins or subtle surveillance, can erode trust and intimacy. This behavior often stems from a fear of unpredictability or loss, but it can push your partner away and create emotional distance.

Parenting is another area where control can manifest strongly. Overscheduling your children's activities, from extracurriculars to playdates, might seem like a way to ensure their success and well-being. However, it can also rob them of the freedom to explore, make mistakes, and develop their interests. Setting rigid rules and expectations can create a high-pressure environment that stifles their creativity and independence. Children may feel like they're constantly under scrutiny, leading to anxiety and a fear of failure.

Understanding how control behaviors permeate daily life is crucial for recognizing their impact. By becoming aware of these tendencies, you can make conscious choices to let go of control, fostering a more balanced and fulfilling life.

The Impact of Control on Mental Health

The link between control behaviors and anxiety is profound. When you constantly strive to control every aspect of your life, it creates a state of hypervigilance. Your mind is always on high alert, scanning for potential problems and planning for every possible outcome. This constant worry can be exhausting. You might find yourself lying awake at night, unable to shut off your thoughts, leading to chronic sleep issues. Physical symptoms often accompany this mental strain —headaches, fatigue, and even digestive problems become your unwelcome companions. The body and mind are in a perpetual state of stress, and it's a heavy burden to carry.

Control behaviors also take a toll on self-esteem. When you set impossibly high standards, and things inevitably fall short, feelings of inadequacy creep in. You might start to believe that you're not good enough, that your worth is somehow tied to your ability to manage everything perfectly. This can lead to imposter syndrome, where you feel like a fraud despite your accomplishments. You might constantly fear being exposed as incapable or unworthy, leading to even more controlled behaviors to mask these insecurities. The cycle is vicious and self-perpetuating, eroding your sense of self-worth bit by bit.

The broader consequences on overall well-being are equally concerning. The relentless pursuit of control puts you at a heightened risk for burnout. You're constantly juggling, always one step away from dropping everything. This chronic stress can sap your energy, leaving you exhausted and emotionally drained. Over time, this can lead to more severe mental health issues such as depression. The joy and spontaneity of life fade away, replaced by a rigid, colorless existence where every moment is planned and every outcome is scrutinized.

Let's talk about real-life impact. Sarah, a dedicated professional in her mid-thirties, was the epitome of success on the outside. She managed her team with an iron grip, ensuring every project met her exacting standards. However, the constant stress took its toll. She began experiencing severe headaches and fatigue, struggling to find motivation. Her relationships with her colleagues became strained as her micromanaging left them feeling undervalued. Eventually, Sarah reached a breaking point, realizing her need for control was unsustainable. Seeking help, she learned to delegate and trust her team, slowly rebuilding her work-life balance and mental health.

Consider Nina, a mother who orchestrated every detail of her family's life. From school projects to family vacations, everything had to be perfect. She believed that by controlling these aspects, she was ensuring the best for her children. However, the constant pressure led to severe anxiety and frequent panic attacks. Nina felt like a failure whenever things didn't go as planned, and her self-esteem plummeted. After a particularly intense episode, she decided to seek therapy. Through counseling, she learned to let go of her need for control, embracing a more flexible approach to parenting. Her mental health improved, and her relationships with her children flourished.

Understanding the impact of control on your mental health is crucial. Recognizing these patterns and their consequences can be the first step toward change. By addressing the root causes and learning to let go, you can reclaim your well-being and live a more balanced, fulfilling life.

How Control Affects Relationships

Control behaviors can wreak havoc on romantic relationships, creating a web of tension and conflict that's hard to untangle. Imagine planning a romantic dinner, only to find yourself micromanaging every detail—from the menu to the seating arrangement—because you believe it's the only way to ensure a perfect evening. This need to control your partner's choices can lead to resentment, even in small matters. Over time, your partner may feel stifled, as though their preferences and autonomy don't matter.

This lack of trust and open communication can breed bitterness and emotional distance, making it difficult for intimacy and genuine connection to flourish.

Friendships aren't immune to the grasp of control either. You might dominate conversations, always steering the topic back to your interests or concerns. This behavior can leave your friends feeling unheard and undervalued, slowly eroding the foundation of your relationship. Dictating group activities, insisting on specific plans, and not allowing others to contribute can further strain these bonds. Friends may start to feel that their opinions and desires are secondary, which can lead to frustration and disengagement. Over time, this can result in a social circle that feels more like a chore than a source of support and joy.

Family dynamics can also suffer under the weight of control behaviors. For instance, constantly correcting your children or setting overly rigid rules can create a high-pressure environment. This strains your relationship with them and can exacerbate sibling rivalry. One child might feel favored or more trusted than the other, leading to jealousy and conflict. In a broader sense, family members might start to feel like they're walking on eggshells, always worried about meeting your high standards. This can create an emotionally charged atmosphere where genuine communication and support are hard to maintain.

Improving these relationships requires consciously letting go of control and fostering mutual respect and trust. One effective strategy is practicing active listening. This means genuinely hearing what the other person is saying without planning your rebuttal or steering the conversation. It's about validating their feelings and showing empathy. Building mutual trust is another crucial element. Trust is a two-way street; it requires both giving and receiving. Show your partner, friends, and family that you trust them by allowing them to make decisions and respecting their choices.

Consider small steps, like letting your partner choose the restaurant for your next date night or allowing your children to decide on a weekend activity. These actions might seem minor, but they send a powerful message of trust and respect. Gradually, these efforts can help mend the strained threads of your relationships, creating a more balanced and fulfilling dynamic.

Self-Assessment: Are You a Control Freak?

One of the most enlightening steps in overcoming control issues is self-awareness. I've designed a self-assessment tool to help you gauge where you stand. This questionnaire will guide you through various aspects of your daily routines, habits, and responses to change.

Let's start with a few questions about your everyday habits:

1. How often do you redo tasks because they weren't done your way?
2. Do you feel anxious when someone else is handling something you usually manage?
3. How do you react when plans change unexpectedly?
4. Are you comfortable delegating tasks to others, or do you prefer to do everything yourself to ensure it's done correctly?

Next, let's consider some scenarios to understand your responses to change:

1. Imagine you've planned a weekend getaway, but sudden weather changes disrupt your plans. How do you handle the situation?
2. Your partner decides to cook dinner but doesn't follow the recipe to the letter. What's your immediate reaction?

3. At work, a project deadline is moved up unexpectedly. What's your first course of action?

Now, let's talk about scoring and interpretation. Each question is designed to reflect a spectrum of control behaviors. You'll score each response on a scale from 1 (rarely) to 5 (always).

Here's a simple scoring rubric:

- 0-15: You exhibit minimal control behaviors.
- 16-30: You have moderate control tendencies.
- 31-45: Your control behaviors are significant and may impact your life and relationships.

Interpreting your score is crucial. A lower score indicates that control isn't a significant issue for you, but staying mindful is worthwhile. A moderate score suggests that while you manage well most of the time, certain triggers can bring out control behaviors. A high score means control is a significant part of your life, and addressing it could lead to healthier relationships and improved well-being.

For personalized feedback, those with high scores will benefit from tailored advice. Focus on small steps to delegate tasks and embrace flexibility. For those with moderate scores, work on identifying specific triggers and developing coping mechanisms. Lower scores should maintain their current balance while remaining vigilant for emerging control behaviors.

Follow-up actions can vary based on your score. Seeking professional help, such as therapy, can benefit high scores. Therapists can provide structured support and techniques tailored to your needs. Engaging in self-help activities is another effective route. Consider mindfulness practices, journaling, or joining support groups focused on reducing control behaviors.

Self-awareness is the cornerstone of change. Understanding your control tendencies allows you to take actionable steps toward a more balanced and fulfilling life. This assessment is just the beginning. Embrace its insights and use them as a foundation for growth and transformation.

TWO

Practical Tools for Immediate Change

Imagine waking up in the morning without the heavy weight of anxiety pressing down on your chest. The day's tasks are still there but feel like a manageable mountain. Instead, you feel a sense of calm and control—not the controlling kind, but the kind that comes from within. This sense of peace might seem elusive, but it's within reach, and mindfulness is a powerful tool to help you get there.

Mindfulness Techniques to Calm the Mind

Mindfulness is about being present in the moment without judgment. It's a simple concept but incredibly powerful in reducing controlling behaviors. At its core, mindfulness means paying attention to what you're doing as you're doing it. When you're mindful, you're fully engaged in the present, which leaves less room for anxious thoughts about the past or future.

The benefits of mindfulness for mental health are well-documented. Studies have shown that mindfulness can reduce symptoms of anxiety and depression, improve concentration, and increase emotional regulation. Practicing mindfulness can break the cycle of overthinking and over-controlling, leading to a more balanced and fulfilling life.

Let's start with some simple mindfulness exercises. One effective technique is the body scan meditation. Find a quiet space where you won't be disturbed. Sit or lie comfortably, close your eyes, and take a few deep breaths. Starting from the top of your head, slowly move your attention down through your body, noticing any sensations without trying to change them. If your mind wanders, gently bring it back to the present moment. This exercise helps you become more aware of your physical sensations, reducing the urge to control your environment.

Another accessible practice is mindful walking. As you walk, focus on the sensation of your feet touching the ground, the movement of your legs, and the rhythm of your breath. Notice your surroundings —the colors, the sounds, the smells—without getting lost in thought. This simple act of walking with awareness can ground you in the present moment and alleviate anxiety.

Incorporating mindfulness into daily routines can make a significant difference. Mindful eating is a great place to start. Instead of rushing through meals, take the time to savor each bite. Notice the flavors, textures, and aromas of your food. Eating mindfully enhances your dining experience and helps you tune into your body's hunger and fullness cues, promoting healthier eating habits.

Mindfulness can also be integrated into household chores. For example, while washing dishes, focus on the sensation of the water, the movement of your hands, and the sound of the clinking dishes. By turning mundane tasks into opportunities for mindfulness, you can transform daily routines into moments of calm and clarity.

Consider the story of Emily, a high-powered executive who used mindfulness to regain control over her life. She started practicing mindfulness during her lunch breaks, taking just ten minutes to focus on her breath and clear her mind. This simple change helped her manage work stress and improved her productivity. She incorporated mindfulness into family time at home, leading to more meaningful connections with her children.

Or take Lisa, a mother of two, who was constantly overwhelmed by her kids' schedules and household responsibilities. She began practicing mindfulness with her children, turning bedtime into a calming ritual of deep breathing and gratitude. This not only reduced her anxiety but also created a peaceful bedtime routine for her kids.

Deep-Breathing Exercises for Instant Stress Relief

Ever notice how a few deep breaths can instantly calm you down? There's science behind it. Deep breathing activates the parasympathetic nervous system, the body's natural way of hitting the "calm down" button. This system slows your heart rate and reduces cortisol—the stress hormone that makes you feel like the sky is falling. When cortisol levels drop, your body and mind relax, making it easier to let go of the need to control every little thing.

Let's start with the box breathing method. This exercise is simple but effective. Find a comfortable seat and close your eyes. Inhale deeply through your nose for a count of four. Hold your breath for another count of four. Exhale slowly through your mouth for four, then hold your breath again for four. Repeat this cycle several times. This method calms your mind and helps you regain focus, making it easier to navigate stressful situations without feeling the need to control them.

Another great technique is the 4-7-8 breathing method. This exercise is beneficial for reducing anxiety and promoting relaxation. Here's how you do it: Sit or lie down comfortably. Close your eyes and inhale quietly through your nose for a count of four. Hold your breath for a count of seven. Then, exhale completely through your mouth, making a whoosh sound for a count of eight. Repeat this cycle three to four times. The 4-7-8 method works by regulating your breath, which helps calm the nervous system, making it easier to let go of control and embrace the present moment.

Incorporating these breathing exercises into your daily routine can make a significant difference. Start your day with a morning breathing ritual. Before getting out of bed, practice the box breathing or 4-7-8 method for a few minutes. This sets a calm tone for the day and prepares you to easily handle whatever comes your way. During work, take short breathing breaks. Set a reminder on your phone or computer to pause for a quick breathing exercise every two hours. This not only helps to reduce stress but also improves focus and productivity.

Consider the story of Jenna, a working woman constantly overwhelmed by workplace demands. She started incorporating the 4-7-8 breathing technique during her lunch breaks. Within weeks, she noticed a significant reduction in her anxiety levels and found it easier to delegate tasks without feeling the need to micromanage. Or think about Maria, a mother of three, who used deep-breathing exercises to calm herself during chaotic mornings. She would take a few minutes to practice box breathing before waking her kids. This simple practice helped her approach the morning rush with a sense of calm, making the whole routine smoother for everyone involved.

Time-Management Tips for a Balanced Life

Effective time management can be a game-changer in reducing the need for control. Managing your time well creates a sense of order and predictability, significantly decreasing anxiety. Poor time management, on the other hand, often leads to chaos and stress, which can trigger controlling behaviors. You might feel like you need to micromanage every detail to keep things from spiraling out of control. Improving your time management skills can create a more balanced and less stressful life.

Prioritization is a key strategy in managing your time effectively. Start by identifying what truly matters to you and focus your energy on those tasks. Make a list of your priorities and rank them in order of importance. This helps you allocate your time and resources more efficiently, ensuring you spend your energy on what truly matters. Time-blocking is another incredibly useful method. This involves dividing your day into blocks of time, each dedicated to a specific task or activity. By setting aside dedicated time for important tasks, you can work more efficiently and avoid the temptation to multitask, which often leads to mistakes and stress.

Several tools and apps can assist you in managing your time more effectively. Popular time-management apps like Trello and Asana offer visual ways to organize tasks and projects. You can create boards for different projects, set deadlines, and track your progress. Digital calendars like Google Calendar can also be incredibly useful. Use them to schedule your tasks, set reminders, and ensure that you allocate time for breaks and self-care. These tools help you stay on track and make it easier to manage your day without feeling overwhelmed.

Consider the case of Laura, a marketing manager who used to feel constantly overwhelmed by her workload. She started using Trello to organize her projects and tasks. She reduced her stress by breaking her to-do list into manageable chunks and setting realistic deadlines. She also used Google Calendar to schedule her tasks and set reminders for important deadlines. This structured approach allowed her to manage her work more efficiently, leaving more time for personal activities and reducing the need to control every detail.

Another example is Sarah, a mother of two who struggled to balance her household duties with her part-time job. She began using a digital calendar to schedule her day, setting aside specific times for work, household chores, and quality time with her children. By creating a structured yet flexible schedule, she managed her responsibilities more effectively, reducing her stress and improving her overall well-being. These examples show how better time management can help you create a more balanced and fulfilling life.

Creating Daily Routines for Flexibility

Establishing flexible routines can be a game-changer in managing control issues. Routines provide a sense of order and predictability, which can significantly reduce anxiety and stress. When you have a routine, you make fewer decisions throughout the day, which reduces decision fatigue. Imagine waking up and knowing exactly what your morning entails without thinking about it. This kind of structure helps to create a sense of stability and control from within rather than needing to control external circumstances.

To design a flexible daily routine, start with your mornings and evenings. Morning routines might include activities like a brief stretch, a healthy breakfast, and a few minutes of journaling or reading. Evening routines can involve winding down with a good book, a relaxing bath, or gentle yoga. The key is to choose activities that set a positive tone for your day and help you unwind at night. Integrate downtime into your schedule to ensure that you have moments to recharge. This can be as simple as a 15-minute coffee break in the afternoon or a short walk after lunch.

Life is unpredictable, and even the best-laid plans can go awry. Adapting routines to unexpected changes is crucial for maintaining flexibility. One effective strategy is to have backup plans in place. For example, if your morning workout gets canceled due to rain, have an indoor exercise routine ready. If a work meeting runs late, have a quick dinner option available to avoid further stress. The goal is to be prepared for disruptions without letting them derail your entire day.

Take the example of Karen, a project manager who used to feel overwhelmed by her packed schedule. She created a flexible work routine that included blocks of time for focused work, short breaks, and buffer periods for unexpected tasks. This approach allowed her to stay productive without feeling stressed. On the other hand, Marie, a mother of three, managed her family's hectic schedule by incorporating flexible routines. She set specific times for homework, play, and family dinners but left room for spontaneous activities. This reduced her stress and made her children feel more relaxed and happy.

Routines are not about rigidity but about creating a framework that supports your well-being. By designing flexible routines, you provide structure while leaving room for life's unpredictability. This balanced approach helps to reduce the need for control, allowing you to navigate your day with greater ease and calm.

Setting Realistic Expectations

Setting realistic expectations is crucial for reducing control behaviors. When you set the bar too high for yourself or others, it creates a constant sense of pressure and stress. Unrealistic expectations often lead to disappointment and frustration, making you feel like you must control everything to meet those lofty standards. This cycle can be exhausting and damaging to your mental health. On the other hand, realistic goal-setting can help you manage your time and energy more effectively, reducing the need for control and allowing you to focus on what truly matters.

The link between unrealistic expectations and stress is well-documented. When you expect perfection from yourself or others, you set yourself up for failure. This constant striving for an unattainable ideal can lead to chronic stress and anxiety. Setting realistic expectations can break this cycle and create a more balanced and fulfilling life. Realistic goals are achievable and provide a sense of accomplishment, boosting your self-esteem and reducing the need for control. They allow you to celebrate your successes without the constant fear of falling short.

One effective strategy for setting realistic goals is the SMART goals framework. SMART stands for Specific, Measurable, Achievable, Relevant, and Time-bound. For example, instead of setting a vague goal like "I want to get fit," a SMART goal would be "I will walk for 30 minutes, five days a week, for the next month." This goal is specific, measurable, achievable, relevant, and time-bound, making tracking your progress and staying motivated easier. Breaking down large tasks into smaller, manageable steps can make your goals more attainable. By focusing on one step at a time, you can avoid feeling overwhelmed and maintain a sense of control without being controlling.

Managing expectations in relationships is equally important. Honest conversations about expectations can help you and your partner understand each other's needs and limitations. Communicating openly and listening actively is essential, as well as showing empathy and understanding. Compromise and flexibility are key components of healthy relationships. You might have to adjust your expectations to accommodate your partner's needs, and they will likely do the same for you. Setting realistic expectations together can create a more supportive and balanced relationship.

Consider the story of Anna, a professional who set realistic career goals to manage her work-life balance. Instead of aiming for a promotion within a year, she focused on improving her skills and taking on challenging projects. This approach allowed her to grow professionally without overwhelming herself. Similarly, Jessica, a parent, set achievable family goals by involving her children. They created a weekly schedule that balanced school, extracurricular activities, and family time. This collaborative approach reduced Jessica's stress and made her children feel more involved and valued.

Setting realistic expectations can create a more balanced and fulfilling life. Whether it's in your career, relationships, or daily routines, realistic goals help you manage your time and energy effectively, reducing the need for control and allowing you to focus on what truly matters.

Quick Wins: Small Changes with Big Impact

Sometimes, making significant changes in your life can feel overwhelming. But what if I told you that small, incremental changes can lead to substantial improvements in reducing control behaviors? This concept is rooted in the Japanese philosophy of kaizen, which means continuous improvement. It's about taking small steps consistently to achieve long-term goals. When you start small, it's easier to maintain momentum and less daunting to implement. These tiny adjustments can accumulate over time, leading to significant positive changes in your life.

One of the benefits of starting small is that it reduces the pressure to be perfect. You don't have to overhaul your entire life in one go. Instead, you can focus on making minor adjustments that are manageable and sustainable. For instance, decluttering your workspace can provide an immediate sense of relief and order. A tidy environment can reduce stress and make it easier to focus on essential tasks. Practicing gratitude journaling is another simple change that can have a profound impact. By jotting down a few things you're grateful for each day, you shift your focus from what's wrong to what's right, fostering a more positive outlook.

Building on small successes is key to achieving larger goals. Making a small change and seeing the benefits creates a sense of accomplishment that motivates you to keep going. Celebrating these small wins is crucial. Whether treating yourself to a favorite snack or taking a short break to enjoy a hobby, acknowledging your progress reinforces positive behavior. Creating a habit loop can also help. This involves identifying a trigger, performing a small action, and rewarding yourself. Over time, this loop becomes ingrained, making it easier to maintain new habits.

Take the example of Rachel, a professional who felt overwhelmed by her workload. She started by decluttering her desk, which made her workspace more inviting and less stressful. This small change boosted her productivity, and she gradually implemented other minor adjustments, like scheduling short breaks and using a task management app. These small tweaks significantly improved her efficiency and reduced her need to control every detail.

Another example is Linda, a parent who struggled with managing her chaotic household. She began by establishing a simple morning routine for her family, which included a quick, five-minute tidy-up session. This minor adjustment reduced the morning rush and set a more positive tone for the day. Encouraged by this success, she made other small changes, like preparing lunches the night before and setting up a family calendar. These small steps collectively reduced her stress and improved the overall harmony at home.

Focusing on small, manageable changes can reduce control behaviors and create a more balanced life. These quick wins provide a sense of accomplishment and build momentum, leading to more significant improvements. Remember, it's not about making drastic changes overnight but about consistent, small steps that lead to lasting transformation.

In the next chapter, we'll explore how enhancing mental health and well-being can further support your efforts to relinquish control and embrace a more fulfilling life.

THREE

Enhancing Mental Health and Well-Being

Visualize yourself in a meeting at work, and suddenly, your mind starts racing. You worry about the presentation you have to give next week, the kids' soccer practice, and even whether you remembered to turn off the stove. Your heart pounds, your palms sweat, and you feel like you are losing control. This is anxiety, and it's a familiar foe for many of us. The good news is that there are powerful tools to manage these feelings, and Cognitive-Behavioral Therapy (CBT) is one of the most effective.

Cognitive-Behavioral Techniques for Anxiety

CBT is a type of therapy that focuses on changing unhelpful thought patterns and behaviors. It's based on the idea that our thoughts, feelings, and behaviors are interconnected. Identifying and altering negative thoughts can change how we feel and act. This therapy can be a game-changer for managing anxiety and reducing control issues.

At its core, CBT involves identifying cognitive distortions, which are irrational or exaggerated thoughts that fuel anxiety and control behaviors. Two common distortions are catastrophizing and black-and-white thinking. Catastrophizing involves imagining the worst possible outcome of a situation, making it seem far worse than it is. For example, if you make a mistake at work, you might think, "I'm going to get fired." On the other hand, black-and-white thinking involves seeing things in extremes—everything is either perfect or a disaster. You might believe everything will fall apart if you can't control every detail.

Cognitive restructuring is a key CBT technique that helps reframe these negative thoughts. Start by identifying a negative thought. Ask yourself what triggered it and how it makes you feel. Next, challenge the thought by examining the evidence for and against it. Is there a more balanced way to view the situation? Finally, replace the negative thought with a more positive or realistic one. For instance, instead of thinking, "I'm going to get fired," you might think, "Everyone makes mistakes; I can learn from this and improve."

Let's look at a real-life application. Consider Emily, a project manager who struggled with anxiety at work. She often felt overwhelmed by the need to control every aspect of her projects. Through CBT, Emily learned to identify her cognitive distortions. She realized she was catastrophizing and expecting perfection from herself and her team. By practicing cognitive restructuring, she challenged these thoughts and replaced them with more realistic ones. She started to see mistakes as opportunities for growth rather than disasters. This shift in mindset helped her reduce her anxiety and become a more effective leader.

Another example is Sarah, a mother who found it hard to relinquish control at home. She worried constantly about her children's safety and well-being, leading to overprotective behaviors. Through CBT, Sarah identified her black-and-white thinking. She believed something terrible would happen if she didn't oversee every detail. By challenging these thoughts and replacing them with more balanced ones, Sarah learned to trust her children's abilities and give them more independence. This not only reduced her anxiety but also improved her relationship with her kids.

CBT provides practical tools to manage anxiety and control issues. You can reframe your thoughts and change how you feel and act by identifying and challenging cognitive distortions. This empowers you to relinquish control and embrace a more balanced, fulfilling life.

Stress-Reduction Methods You Can Start Today

Managing stress is crucial for reducing control behaviors because chronic stress wreaks havoc on your mental health. When you're constantly stressed, your body is in a perpetual state of fight-or-flight, which can lead to anxiety, depression, and even physical health issues like high blood pressure. The link between stress and control is evident: the more stressed you are, the more you feel the need to control your surroundings to create a sense of stability. But this creates a vicious cycle, as the need for control often adds to your stress rather than alleviating it.

Chronic stress impacts your mental health in profound ways. It can make you feel constantly on edge, affect your concentration, and even alter your mood, making you more irritable and less patient. This means you're more likely to react impulsively, get overwhelmed easily, and resort to controlling behaviors to regain a sense of order. Understanding this connection is the first step toward breaking the cycle.

Simple stress-reduction techniques can make a significant difference. One effective method is progressive muscle relaxation. This involves tensing and slowly releasing each muscle group, starting from your toes and working your way up to your head. By focusing on the physical sensations, you can divert your mind from stressors and achieve a state of relaxation. Guided imagery is another powerful tool. Close your eyes and imagine yourself in a peaceful setting—like a beach or a forest. Engage all your senses to make the scene as vivid as possible. This mental escape can help lower your stress levels and give you a break from the pressures of daily life.

Incorporating stress reduction into your daily routines is easier than you think. Set aside dedicated time each day for relaxation activities. This could be as simple as a 10-minute meditation session in the morning or a short walk during your lunch break. Creating a stress-free environment at home also helps. Declutter your living space, play calming music, and use essential oils like lavender or chamomile to create a soothing atmosphere. These small changes can make your home a sanctuary where you can unwind and recharge.

Consider the story of Lisa, a marketing executive who felt overwhelmed by her demanding job. She started incorporating stress-reduction techniques into her workday, like taking short breaks to practice deep breathing and using guided imagery during lunch breaks. These small adjustments helped her manage her stress and improved her productivity. Similarly, Maria, a mother of two, used stress management techniques to improve her family dynamics. She introduced progressive muscle relaxation exercises before bedtime, turning them into a family activity. This reduced her stress and created a calming routine for her children, improving their sleep and overall mood.

By understanding the importance of stress management and incorporating simple yet effective techniques into your daily life, you can break the stress and control cycle and lead a more balanced and fulfilling life.

The Importance of Sleep and Rest

Quality sleep affects your mental health in profound ways. When you sleep well, your brain can restore and rejuvenate. This process is crucial for emotional regulation and overall mental well-being. On the flip side, poor sleep can exacerbate anxiety and make you feel more out of control. The next day feels like a battle on nights when you toss and turn. Your patience wears thin, and your ability to handle stress diminishes.

There's a strong connection between sleep and anxiety. When you're sleep-deprived, your body produces more cortisol, the stress hormone. Elevated cortisol levels can increase feelings of anxiety and make it harder to manage everyday stressors. Additionally, lack of sleep impairs your brain's ability to regulate emotions, leading to heightened irritability and mood swings. This emotional volatility can make you feel more out of control, perpetuating a cycle of anxiety and poor sleep.

Improving sleep quality can be a game-changer. Start by establishing a bedtime routine that signals your body it's time to wind down. This might include reading a book, taking a warm bath, or practicing gentle stretching. Consistency is key—try to go to bed and wake up at the same time every day, even on weekends. Creating a sleep-friendly environment also helps. Make sure your bedroom is cool, dark, and quiet. Consider using blackout curtains, earplugs, or a white noise machine to eliminate disruptions.

Common sleep issues can throw a wrench in your plans for better rest. Insomnia, characterized by difficulty falling or staying asleep, is a frequent culprit. If you struggle with insomnia, try relaxation techniques like progressive muscle relaxation or mindfulness meditation before bed. Another issue is sleep apnea, where breathing repeatedly stops and starts during sleep. If you suspect sleep apnea, consult a healthcare professional for proper diagnosis and treatment.

A CPAP machine or lifestyle changes like weight loss can make a significant difference.

Improved sleep can yield remarkable benefits. Take the story of Megan, who struggled with insomnia for years. She prioritized her sleep hygiene by establishing a consistent bedtime routine and calming environment. Within weeks, she noticed a significant reduction in her anxiety levels and felt more in control of her daily life. Another example is Jessica, a busy professional who balanced work and sleep. She used to burn the midnight oil, believing that sacrificing sleep was the only way to stay on top of her workload. After prioritizing sleep, she found that her productivity improved, and she was better equipped to handle stress.

Sleep is a powerful tool for enhancing mental health and reducing control behaviors. By prioritizing quality rest, you can improve emotional regulation, reduce anxiety, and create a more balanced, fulfilling life.

Nutrition and Its Impact on Mental Health

Imagine feeling more balanced and less anxious simply by adjusting what you eat. Nutrition profoundly affects your mental well-being and control behaviors. A balanced diet can stabilize mood, increase energy levels, and make it easier to manage stress. Specific nutrients play critical roles in mental health. For instance, omega-3 fatty acids, found in fish like salmon and walnuts, reduce symptoms of depression and anxiety. These nutrients help regulate neurotransmitters, chemicals in your brain that influence mood.

Incorporating a variety of fruits and vegetables into your diet is another powerful way to boost mental health. These foods are rich in antioxidants, vitamins, and minerals that support brain function. Leafy greens like spinach and kale are especially beneficial, as they contain folate, which helps produce neurotransmitters like serotonin and dopamine. These chemicals are often called the "feel-good" neurotransmitters because they help regulate mood and emotion. You can create a more stable and positive mental state by nourishing your brain with these essential nutrients.

While it's tempting to reach for sugary snacks or caffeinated beverages when you're stressed, these can exacerbate anxiety and control issues. Sugar can cause rapid spikes and drops in blood sugar levels, leading to mood swings and increased feelings of anxiety. High sugar consumption has also been linked to inflammation, negatively affecting brain function. Similarly, caffeine in coffee, tea, and many soft drinks can increase heart rate and make you feel jittery. For some, this heightened state of alertness can trigger anxiety and make it harder to manage stress.

Consider Jessica, a busy professional who used to rely on coffee and sugary snacks to get through her hectic days. She noticed that her anxiety levels were through the roof, and she was constantly on edge. After reading about the impact of diet on mental health, she decided to make some changes. Jessica started incorporating more omega-3-rich foods like salmon and walnuts into her meals. She also added a variety of colorful fruits and vegetables to her diet, focusing on leafy greens. Within weeks, she felt more balanced and less anxious. Her mood stabilized, and she found it easier to manage her workload without feeling overwhelmed.

Another example is Grace, a mother of two who struggled with mood swings and irritability. She realized her diet was high in sugar and caffeine, likely contributing to her emotional rollercoaster. Grace decided to cut back on sugary snacks and limit her caffeine intake. She replaced them with healthier options like fresh fruit, herbal teas, and whole grains. The change in her diet had a noticeable impact on her mental health. She felt more in control of her emotions and could handle the daily parenting challenges better.

By understanding the connection between diet and mental health, you can make informed choices that positively impact your well-being. Small changes in your eating habits can significantly improve mood, energy levels, and your ability to manage stress and anxiety.

Exercise as a Tool for Emotional Balance

Exercise is a potent ally in the quest for emotional balance and mental health. When you engage in physical activity, your body releases endorphins, often called "feel-good" hormones. These natural chemicals act as painkillers and mood elevators, reducing stress and fostering a sense of well-being. Regular exercise also helps lower cortisol levels. This dual action—boosting endorphins and reducing cortisol—creates a more balanced emotional state, making it easier to manage anxiety and control behaviors.

Incorporating exercise into your daily routine doesn't have to be a daunting task. Start with activities that you enjoy and can easily fit into your schedule. Walking, jogging, and cycling are excellent options that don't require special equipment or memberships. Yoga and Pilates are particularly beneficial for mental health as they combine physical movement with mindfulness and breathing techniques. Strength training and aerobic exercises also release endorphins and reduce stress. The key is finding a balance that works for you—mixing different exercises can keep things interesting and engage various muscle groups.

Finding time for exercise can be challenging, especially with a busy schedule. One common barrier is the lack of time. However, you can overcome this by breaking your exercise routine into shorter sessions spread throughout the day. Even a 10-minute walk during your lunch break or a quick yoga session in the morning can make a significant difference. Physical limitations can also pose a challenge. If you have mobility issues or chronic pain, consider low-impact exercises like swimming or chair yoga. The goal is to move in a way that feels good for your body and mind.

Real-life stories provide powerful motivation. Take the example of Rachel, a marketing executive who used exercise to manage her workplace stress. She started incorporating short, brisk walks during her breaks, gradually building up to longer weekend hikes. This simple change improved her physical health and helped her clear her mind and return to work with renewed focus. Another inspiring story is that of Lisa, a busy mother who found creative ways to include her kids in her exercise routine. She turned weekend park visits into family fitness sessions, where they would play games, run around, and even do yoga together. This helped Lisa manage her stress and fostered a healthy, active lifestyle for her children.

Exercise is a versatile tool that significantly enhances emotional balance and mental health. You can create a more balanced, fulfilling life by finding activities you enjoy, overcoming common barriers, and incorporating movement into your daily routine.

Incorporating Meditation into Your Daily Routine

Meditation is a practice that involves focusing your mind and eliminating distractions to achieve a state of relaxation and mental clarity. By dedicating time to meditating, you can significantly reduce anxiety and the urge to control everything around you. The beauty of meditation lies in its simplicity and the profound impact it can have on your mental health. It's a tool that helps you stay grounded, become more aware of your thoughts, and respond to life's challenges with a calm mind.

One of the most accessible forms of meditation is breathing meditation. Sit comfortably, close your eyes, and focus on your breath. Inhale deeply through your nose, hold for a moment, and then exhale slowly through your mouth. Pay attention to the sensation of the breath entering and leaving your body. If your mind wanders, gently bring your focus back to your breath. This practice helps center your thoughts and reduces stress by promoting relaxation.

Another effective technique is the body scan meditation. Lie down or sit comfortably, close your eyes, and take a few deep breaths. Starting from your toes, slowly move your attention up through your body, noticing any tension or discomfort. As you focus on each body part, consciously relax those muscles. This practice helps you become more in tune with your body and alleviates physical tension, contributing to overall mental well-being.

Making meditation a regular habit can be transformative. To integrate meditation into your daily routine, set a specific time each day for your practice. Consistency is key, whether first thing in the morning or right before bed. Creating a peaceful meditation space can also enhance your practice. Choose a quiet spot in your home where you feel comfortable and free from distractions. Adding elements like candles, soft lighting, or calming music can create a serene atmosphere that encourages relaxation.

Consider the story of Rebecca, a high-stakes lawyer who struggled with constant stress and anxiety. She began incorporating meditation into her daily routine, starting with just five minutes each morning. Over time, she extended her practice to 20 minutes, finding that it helped her manage work stress and improve her focus. Her colleagues even noticed a positive change in her demeanor and productivity. On the home front, Emily, a mother of three, introduced meditation to her children. They practiced together before bedtime, turning it into a calming family ritual. This improved Emily's mental health and created a peaceful bedtime routine for her kids, enhancing their emotional well-being.

Meditation offers a simple yet powerful way to reduce anxiety and manage control behaviors. Dedicating a few minutes daily to this practice can cultivate inner peace and resilience, allowing you to navigate life's challenges more easily. Whether you're a busy professional or a parent juggling multiple responsibilities, meditation can be a valuable addition to your mental health toolkit.

Enhancing mental health and well-being through these practices sets a solid foundation for personal growth. As we move forward, we'll delve into understanding control behaviors and how they manifest in various aspects of your life.

FOUR

Deep Self-Reflection and Awareness

Picture yourself sitting in a cozy nook with a cup of tea, a blank journal, and a pen poised to capture your thoughts. It's a quiet moment amidst the whirlwind of your busy life. This scenario might seem idyllic, but it's a powerful practice that can lead to profound self-discovery. Journaling is more than just putting pen to paper; it's a gateway to understanding your control behaviors and uncovering the root causes of your need for control.

Journaling enhances self-awareness by allowing you to explore your thoughts and feelings in a structured way. When you jot down your experiences, you gain clarity and insight into your behavior patterns. This process can help you identify triggers and understand why you react the way you do. Journaling also provides an emotional release, offering a safe space to express your frustrations, fears, and hopes. As you pour your thoughts onto the page, you lighten the mental load, making it easier to manage stress and control tendencies.

To get started, consider these guided journaling prompts designed to help you explore your control tendencies. First, describe a recent situation where you felt the need to control. What were your thoughts and feelings? Reflecting on specific instances can help you identify patterns and triggers. Next, ask yourself, "What are your biggest fears about losing control?" This question encourages you to dig deep and uncover the underlying anxieties that drive your need for control. By addressing these fears, you can begin to develop healthier coping mechanisms.

Different journaling techniques can keep the practice engaging and effective. Stream-of-consciousness writing is continuously writing without worrying about grammar or punctuation. This free-flowing style helps you tap into your subconscious mind, revealing thoughts and feelings you might not know. Gratitude journaling is another powerful technique. Each day, write down three things you're grateful for. Focusing on positive aspects of your life can shift your mindset from control and perfectionism to appreciation and contentment.

Consider the story of Laura, a professional who used journaling for emotional insight. Laura started journaling after feeling overwhelmed by her demanding job. Through her entries, she realized that her need to control every project stemmed from a fear of failure. By acknowledging this fear, Laura began to delegate tasks and trust her team, significantly reducing her stress levels. Another example is Jillian, a mother who felt pressured to be the perfect parent. Journaling helped her see that societal expectations drove her need for control. By recognizing this, Jillian learned to set realistic expectations for herself and her children, improving her relationship with them.

Guided Journaling Prompts:

1. Describe a recent situation where you felt the need to control. What were your thoughts and feelings?
2. What are your biggest fears related to losing control?

3. Write about a time when you let go of control, and things turned out better than expected.

Engaging in these practices can lead to significant personal growth and emotional healing. By making journaling a regular part of your routine, you can gain deeper insights into your behavior, reduce anxiety, and foster a more balanced and fulfilling life.

Reflective Questions to Uncover Hidden Anxieties

Reflective questioning is a powerful tool for uncovering hidden anxieties that drive your control behaviors. Asking yourself deep, reflective questions can help you identify underlying fears and gain insight into subconscious thoughts. These questions act as mirrors, reflecting the hidden parts of your psyche that you might not be fully aware of. This introspection aims to bring these hidden elements into the light, allowing you to understand and address them.

One key benefit of reflective questioning is the identification of underlying fears. For many of us, control behaviors are rooted in a fear of uncertainty, failure, or inadequacy. By asking yourself targeted questions, you can unearth these fears and understand how they influence your actions. Another significant benefit is insight into subconscious thoughts. Subconscious beliefs and patterns often drive the need for control we might not recognize consciously. Reflective questioning helps bring these hidden thoughts to the surface, allowing you to examine them critically.

Consider asking yourself specific questions designed to prompt introspection and reveal hidden anxieties. Start with, "What do you fear might happen if you lose control?" This question encourages you to confront your worst-case scenarios and examine the fears that drive your need for control. Another powerful question is, "How does the need for perfection impact your daily life?" Reflecting on this can help you understand the toll perfectionism takes on your mental and emotional well-being. These questions are not about finding immediate solutions but gaining a deeper understanding of your inner world.

It is crucial to approach these questions honestly and thoughtfully. Take your time to reflect before writing your answers. Find a quiet space where you can be alone with your thoughts, free from distractions. Be honest with yourself and nonjudgmental. Remember, this is a safe space for exploration, not criticism. Allow yourself to feel any emotions and write them down without censoring yourself. This process can be uncomfortable, but it's a necessary step towards self-awareness and change.

Reflective questioning has led to significant breakthroughs for many individuals. Take the story of Shari, a mother who constantly needed to control every aspect of her children's lives. Through reflective questioning, she uncovered a deep-seated fear of inadequacy stemming from her childhood experiences. Recognizing this fear allowed Shari to let go of some of her control behaviors and trust her children more. Similarly, Jamie, a professional, struggled with a relentless need for perfection at work. Reflecting on the question, "What do you fear might happen if you lose control?" helped her realize that her fear of failure was driving her perfectionism. This insight enabled Jamie to set more realistic expectations and reduce her stress.

Reflective questioning is a journey into the depths of your psyche. By asking yourself the right questions and approaching them honestly and with compassion, you can uncover hidden anxieties and address the fears that drive your need for control. This process is not about finding immediate solutions but gaining a deeper understanding of your inner world. Through this self-awareness, you can make meaningful changes, reduce control behaviors, and foster a more balanced and fulfilling existence.

Understanding Your Triggers

Triggers are the emotional catalysts that drive our control behaviors, often without us even realizing it. An emotional trigger is any event or situation that evokes a strong emotional response, usually tied to past experiences or ingrained fears. Common triggers for control tendencies include unpredictable situations, relationships that challenge your sense of security, or even certain environments that remind you of past failures. Recognizing these triggers is crucial for managing control behaviors effectively.

To identify your triggers, start by keeping a trigger journal. Whenever you need to control a situation, jot down the specifics: What happened? How did you feel? What thoughts ran through your mind? Over time, patterns will emerge, helping you pinpoint what sets off your need for control. Note both your physical and emotional responses. Do you feel your heart rate increase? Do your thoughts race? These physical cues can be just as telling as your emotional reactions.

Once you've identified your triggers, managing them becomes the next step. Grounding techniques can be beneficial. These simple methods bring you back to the present moment, helping you regain control over your emotional state. One effective technique is the "5-4-3-2-1" method: Identify five things you can see, four things you can touch, three things you can hear, two things you can smell, and one thing you can taste. Another strategy is to develop a trigger action plan. This involves creating a step-by-step plan for how to respond when you encounter a trigger. For example, if a sudden change in plans sets you off, your action plan might include taking deep breaths, reminding yourself that things are okay to be imperfect, and then calmly addressing the change.

Real-life examples can illustrate how identifying and managing triggers can lead to significant improvements. Take the case of Emily, a professional who found that last-minute changes at work triggered her need to micromanage her team. By keeping a trigger journal, she realized that her anxiety stemmed from a fear of appearing incompetent. With this insight, she developed a trigger action plan that included grounding techniques and open communication with her team about her concerns. This approach reduced her stress and improved her relationships at work.

Another example is Terri, a parent who felt overwhelmed whenever her children's routines were disrupted. She noted her physical responses—tight chest and clenched fists—and used grounding techniques to calm herself. Terri also developed a trigger action plan, which included taking a moment to breathe, reassuring herself that flexibility is healthy for her children, and calmly addressing the situation. This strategy helped her manage her triggers more effectively, creating a more harmonious family environment.

By understanding and managing your triggers, you can gain control over your emotional responses rather than letting them control you. This reduces the urge to micromanage and over-control and fosters healthier relationships and a more balanced life.

The Role of Past Experiences

Our past experiences, especially childhood ones, can profoundly shape our control behaviors. Imagine growing up in an environment where unpredictability was the norm. Perhaps your parents were inconsistent in their rules, or maybe you faced trauma like neglect or abuse. These early experiences can create a deep-seated need for control to cope with uncertainty and fear. The influence of childhood trauma on your present behavior can be significant. If you were often left to fend for yourself or felt unsafe, you might have developed control behaviors as a survival mechanism. These patterns can persist into adulthood, affecting your relationships and daily life.

Past relationships also play a crucial role. Consider a previous relationship where you constantly felt undermined or invalidated. Such experiences can lead to an ingrained belief that you must control your environment to protect yourself. This is particularly true if you've had relationships that were emotionally or physically abusive. The impact of these past relationships can linger, making it difficult to trust others and let go of control. Reflecting on these experiences can provide valuable insights into why you may need to control situations and people in your current life.

To explore your past, write a timeline of significant life events. Note down moments that were particularly impactful, both positive and negative. Reflect on how these experiences shaped your need for control. Ask yourself questions like, "How did my childhood environment influence my behavior today?" or "What past relationships have contributed to my current need for control?" This exercise can help you connect the dots between your past and present, offering a clearer understanding of your behavior. Reflecting on past relationships and their impact can also be enlightening. Consider your interactions with significant people and how these relationships might have influenced your control tendencies.

Healing from past experiences involves several strategies. Seeking therapy or counseling can be incredibly beneficial. A trained professional can guide you through unpacking your past and developing healthier coping mechanisms. Therapy provides a safe space to explore your feelings and gain insights into your behavior. Practicing self-compassion and forgiveness is another crucial aspect of healing. Be kind to yourself as you reflect on your past. Understand that your control behaviors were likely developed to protect yourself. Forgive yourself for any perceived shortcomings and acknowledge your strength in seeking change.

Consider the story of Emma, a professional who grew up with a controlling parent. Emma realized that her need to control every detail at work stemmed from her childhood experiences. Through therapy, she learned to set boundaries and trust her team, significantly reducing her stress levels. Another example is Maria, a mother who faced childhood trauma. She often felt the need to micromanage her children's lives to ensure their safety. Through counseling and self-compassion, Maria learned to let go of her control tendencies and foster a more trusting relationship with her children.

Identifying Fear-Based Thoughts

Fear-based thoughts are those nagging voices in your head that stem from deep-seated anxieties and insecurities. They often arise from past experiences and can heavily influence your behavior, especially your need to control. These thoughts are usually negative, irrational, and exaggerated, making you feel like you must manage every little detail to prevent disaster. Characteristics of fear-based thinking include catastrophizing, where you always imagine the worst-case scenario, and black-and-white thinking, which makes you see situations in extremes.

Common fear-based thoughts related to control might include, "If I don't oversee this project, it will fail," or "If I don't plan every detail of this event, it will be a disaster." These thoughts create a sense of urgency and anxiety, driving you to micromanage situations. They can make you feel you must be perfect to avoid criticism or failure.

To identify these fear-based thoughts, start by keeping a thought journal. Write down your thoughts whenever you feel anxious or have the urge to control. Another helpful tool is a thought record worksheet, where you can document the situation, thoughts, emotions, and an alternative, more balanced thought. This exercise helps you see patterns in your thinking and understand the root of your anxiety.

The next step is challenging and reframing these thoughts. Cognitive restructuring techniques can be incredibly effective. Start by questioning the validity of your fear-based thoughts. Ask yourself, "Is this thought based on facts or assumptions?" and "What evidence do I have that supports or contradicts this thought?" Replace the negative thought with a more balanced one. For example, change "If I don't do it, it will fail" to "I can trust others to handle this task competently."

Positive affirmations can also help reframe your mindset. Create a list of affirmations that counteract your fear-based thoughts. For instance, if you often think, "I must be perfect to be valued," replace it with "I am worthy and valuable as I am." Repeat these affirmations daily to reinforce a more positive and balanced perspective.

Consider the story of Nora, a professional who constantly fears failure. She believed she would be seen as incompetent if she didn't control every aspect of her work. Nora identified and challenged her fear-based thoughts by keeping a thought journal and using cognitive restructuring. She replaced them with affirmations like, "I am competent and capable," which helped her delegate tasks and reduce her stress.

Another example is Grace, a parent who struggled with feelings of inadequacy. She feared her children would fail if she didn't control their activities. Through thought journaling and positive affirmations, Grace learned to trust her children's abilities, giving them more independence. This not only reduced her anxiety but also improved her relationship with her children.

Building Self-Awareness Through Reflection

Self-awareness is like a flashlight in a dark room—it illuminates those hidden corners of your mind where control behaviors often lurk. Understanding why you act as you do is the first step in making meaningful changes. When you're self-aware, you're better equipped to recognize your emotional triggers and understand the impact of your actions on yourself and others. This heightened awareness helps you regulate your emotions more effectively, reducing the need for control. Think about it: when you know what sets you off, you can take proactive steps to manage your reactions instead of letting them control you.

Increased self-awareness has numerous benefits. It enhances emotional regulation, making staying calm and composed in stressful situations easier. You become more empathetic, understanding your feelings and those of others. This improved empathy can lead to healthier relationships, as you're better able to navigate conflicts and communicate effectively. Additionally, self-awareness fosters personal growth by helping you identify areas for improvement and set realistic goals. It's like having a roadmap for your emotional and mental well-being.

To cultivate self-awareness, try incorporating reflective exercises into your routine. A daily reflection practice can be incredibly beneficial. At the end of each day, take a few minutes to think about your actions and emotions. Ask yourself questions like, "What triggered my need for control today?" and "How did I handle it?" Another powerful tool is mindfulness meditation. This practice involves focusing on the present moment and observing your thoughts and feelings without judgment. Over time, mindfulness can help you become more attuned to your inner world, making it easier to recognize and address control behaviors.

Integrating reflection into daily life doesn't have to be complicated. Set aside specific times for reflection, whether a few minutes each morning or a more extended session at the end of the week. Creating a reflection journal can also be helpful. Use it to jot down your thoughts, feelings, and insights as they arise. This practice helps you track your progress and provides a tangible record of your journey towards greater self-awareness. The key is consistency. Regular reflection lets you stay connected to your inner self, making recognizing and changing control behaviors easier.

Consider the story of Amelia, a professional who struggled with decision-making at work. By setting aside time for daily reflection, Amelia could identify patterns in her behavior. She realized her need for control stemmed from a fear of making mistakes. With this insight, Amelia began to trust her judgment more and delegate tasks to her team, improving her decision-making process and reducing her stress levels. Another example is Lindsay, a mother who used reflection to enhance her parenting. Through regular reflection, Lindsay noticed that her children's unpredictability triggered her control behaviors. By becoming more aware of her reactions, she learned to embrace flexibility, creating a more harmonious home environment.

Building self-awareness through reflection is a powerful way to reduce control behaviors and promote personal growth. By understanding your emotional triggers and recognizing the impact of your actions, you can make meaningful changes that lead to a more balanced, fulfilling life.

FIVE

Improving Relationship Dynamics

Visualize yourself sitting at the dinner table with your partner, but instead of enjoying the meal, you're mentally reviewing the day's events and what still needs to be done. You're so engrossed in your thoughts that you miss the subtle cues that your partner needs to talk. The silence stretches, and soon, both of you are feeling disconnected. This scenario is all too common, highlighting the critical role of effective communication in maintaining healthy relationships.

Effective Communication Skills

Clear communication is the bedrock of any strong relationship. When you communicate effectively, you reduce misunderstandings and build stronger connections with those around you. Clear and honest communication ensures you and your partner feel understood and valued. When you express your thoughts and emotions openly, it fosters an environment of trust and intimacy. Conversely, poor communication can lead to a breakdown in trust and create emotional distance. Misunderstandings can fester, turning minor issues into significant conflicts that strain your relationship.

So, how do you practice clear and honest communication? One essential technique is using "I" statements to express your feelings. Instead of saying, "You never listen to me," try, "I feel unheard when we talk." This approach focuses on your emotions rather than blaming your partner, making it easier for them to understand and empathize with your perspective. Balancing speaking and listening is equally important. Ensure you give your partner the space to express their thoughts and feelings without interruption. This balance creates a dialogue rather than a monologue, fostering mutual respect and understanding.

Non-verbal communication also plays a significant role in how your message is received. Your body language, facial expressions, and tone of voice can reinforce or contradict your words. For instance, crossing your arms while saying, "I'm not upset," sends mixed signals. Aligning your verbal and non-verbal messages is crucial for clear communication. Pay attention to your partner's non-verbal cues as well. Are they avoiding eye contact or clenching their fists? These signs can provide valuable insights into their emotional state, helping you respond empathetically.

To improve your communication skills, consider practicing active listening. This involves fully focusing on the speaker, understanding their message, and responding thoughtfully. A practical exercise is to have a conversation where you only listen and then paraphrase what your partner said to ensure you understood correctly. Another useful exercise is role-playing different communication scenarios. For example, practice discussing a common conflict with your partner and taking turns to express your feelings using "I" statements and active listening techniques. This practice can make real-life conversations smoother and more productive.

Effective communication involves speaking clearly, actively listening, and interpreting nonverbal cues. By practicing these skills, you can build stronger, more intimate relationships, reduce misunderstandings, and create a more harmonious environment in your personal and professional life.

Building Trust with Your Partner

Trust is the cornerstone of any healthy relationship. It's built on honesty, reliability, and emotional safety. When you trust your partner, you feel secure in the relationship, knowing they will be there for you, come what may. Consistency and reliability are crucial elements in building trust. When your partner consistently follows through on their promises, it reinforces the belief that they are dependable. This reliability forms the bedrock of trust, allowing you to feel safe and secure in the relationship. On the other hand, inconsistency and broken promises can erode trust, leaving you uncertain and anxious.

Vulnerability also plays a significant role in building trust. When you allow yourself to be vulnerable with your partner, you open up about your fears, insecurities, and dreams. This openness fosters a deeper connection, showing that you trust your partner enough to share your thoughts and feelings. This encourages your partner to be vulnerable with you, creating a cycle of mutual trust and understanding. The more you share, the stronger your bond becomes, paving the way for a more intimate and trusting relationship.

Rebuilding trust after it has been damaged requires patience and effort from both partners. One of the first steps is acknowledging mistakes and apologizing sincerely. A heartfelt apology shows that you recognize the hurt caused and are willing to make amends. It's important to be specific about what you're apologizing for and to express genuine remorse. Setting and respecting boundaries is another crucial step in rebuilding trust. Boundaries create a sense of safety and respect, making both partners feel secure. By clearly defining what is acceptable and what is not, you create a framework for rebuilding trust.

To foster mutual trust, practice transparency and openness. Share your thoughts and feelings honestly, without fear of judgment. This openness encourages your partner to do the same, creating a more authentic and trusting relationship. Engaging in trust-building activities together can also help strengthen your bond. Consider activities that require cooperation and mutual support, such as team sports, cooking a meal together, or embarking on a new hobby. These activities provide opportunities to demonstrate reliability and trustworthiness, reinforcing the trust in your relationship.

Take the story of Amy and Mark, a couple who faced a breach of trust when Mark was unfaithful. They decided to rebuild their relationship by attending couples therapy, where they learned to communicate openly and set clear boundaries. Mark consistently showed his commitment to change; over time, Amy began to trust him again. Another example is Wendy and Ed, who fostered trust through shared experiences. They started a new hobby together—gardening—which required teamwork and patience. Through this shared activity, they learned to rely on each other, strengthening their trust and deepening their bond.

Navigating Conflicts Without Control

Conflicts in relationships are as inevitable as the changing seasons. They arise from differences in perspectives, unmet needs, or even simple misunderstandings. While conflicts can be uncomfortable, they also offer opportunities for growth and deeper understanding. Imagine a scenario where you and your partner disagree on how to spend your weekend. You want to relax at home, while they prefer an outdoor adventure. This seemingly minor conflict can escalate if handled poorly. However, if approached with an open mind, it can lead to a compromise that satisfies both parties and strengthens your bond.

Financial disagreements, differing parenting styles, and unmet emotional needs are common sources of relationship conflict. These conflicts often stem from underlying issues such as stress, insecurity, or past experiences. Viewing conflicts as opportunities for understanding can shift your perspective. Instead of seeing them as threats, consider them chances to learn more about your partner's needs and values. This mindset can transform conflicts into constructive dialogues, fostering mutual respect and empathy.

When it comes to resolving conflicts, collaborative problem-solving techniques are invaluable. Start by identifying the issue and expressing your feelings without assigning blame. For instance, instead of saying, "You always spend too much money," try, "I feel anxious when our spending exceeds our budget." This approach opens the door to a more productive conversation. Next, brainstorm solutions together. Encourage each other to suggest possible compromises and evaluate them without judgment. The goal is to find a middle ground that works for both parties.

Using a calm and respectful tone during disagreements is crucial. Heated arguments often lead to hurtful words and emotional scars. Practice taking deep breaths and pausing before responding. This helps you stay grounded and prevents knee-jerk reactions. Recognize your emotional triggers and address them. If you feel your anger rising, step away from the conversation to cool down. This break can provide the clarity needed to continue the discussion with a clear mind.

Consider the story of Dorothy and Robert, who frequently clashed over household chores. Dorothy felt overwhelmed by the workload, while Robert believed he was contributing enough. Instead of letting the conflict fester, they decided to approach it collaboratively. They sat down and listed all the household tasks, then divided them based on their strengths and availability. This exercise not only resolved their conflict but also strengthened their partnership. Another example is Megan and Josh, who disagreed on how to discipline their children. By calmly discussing their concerns and finding a compromise, they created a consistent and effective approach to parenting.

Navigating conflicts without control involves emotional regulation and a willingness to understand your partner's perspective. By staying calm and open-minded, you can turn conflicts into opportunities for growth and deeper connection.

The Power of Active Listening

Active listening is a game-changer in any relationship. It means fully focusing on the speaker, understanding their message, and responding thoughtfully. Active listening goes beyond just hearing words; it involves paying attention to the speaker's emotions, body language, and underlying messages. When you practice active listening, you show your partner they are valued and understood, which is crucial for building trust and fostering a deep connection.

Characteristics of active listening include maintaining eye contact, nodding in acknowledgment, and responding with appropriate facial expressions. It also means avoiding interruptions and giving the speaker your undivided attention. These actions create a safe, open space where both partners feel heard and respected. The benefits of active listening are immense, as it builds trust, enhances understanding, and strengthens the emotional bond between partners.

To practice active listening, start with reflective listening and paraphrasing. When your partner speaks, reflect their words to them to show that you understand. For example, if they say, "I'm frustrated with work," you might respond, "It sounds like you're stressed about your job." This technique validates their feelings and encourages them to share more. Asking open-ended questions is another effective method. Instead of yes-or-no questions, ask ones that invite detailed responses, such as, "What do you think could help with your work stress?" This approach fosters a deeper conversation and shows genuine interest in their thoughts and feelings.

Listening barriers can hinder effective communication. Distractions and multitasking are common obstacles. You're not fully present if you're checking your phone or thinking about your to-do list while your partner is talking. Make a conscious effort to eliminate distractions and focus solely on the conversation. Prejudgments and assumptions are another barrier. You're less likely to listen openly if you enter a conversation with preconceived notions about what your partner will say. Approach each conversation with an open mind, ready to hear their perspective without judgment.

Try practical exercises like reflective listening with a partner to enhance your active listening skills. Take turns speaking and listening, practicing reflecting and paraphrasing each other's words. This exercise helps you become more attuned to your partner's emotions and messages. Role-playing different listening scenarios is another valuable practice. Create scenarios where one partner shares a concern and the other practices active listening techniques. This exercise can improve your ability to navigate real-life conversations and conflicts with empathy and understanding.

Active listening is a powerful tool that enhances communication and deepens connections in relationships. You can foster a more supportive and understanding relationship by practicing reflective listening, asking open-ended questions, and overcoming listening barriers. Remember, the goal is to hear the words, truly understand, and connect with your partner more deeply.

Setting Healthy Boundaries

Setting and respecting boundaries is the backbone of any healthy relationship. Boundaries define where one person ends and another begins, providing clarity and mutual respect. They act as invisible lines, protecting your emotional space and ensuring you feel safe and valued. When boundaries are respected, they foster emotional safety and trust, creating a relationship where both partners feel secure and understood. Without boundaries, relationships can become chaotic and stressful, leading to resentment and emotional burnout.

The connection between boundaries and respect is profound. When you establish clear boundaries, you communicate your needs and limits, which fosters mutual respect. Your partner understands what is acceptable and what is not, reducing misunderstandings and conflicts. This clarity helps build a foundation of trust, as both partners feel confident that their boundaries will be honored. Emotional safety is another critical aspect. Boundaries create a safe space to express yourself without fear of judgment or intrusion. This emotional safety is essential for deepening intimacy and connection.

To set effective boundaries, start by identifying your limits. Reflect on what makes you feel uncomfortable or stressed in your relationship. These feelings are often indicators of where boundaries are needed. Once you've identified your boundaries, communicate them assertively. Use clear and direct language to express your needs. For example, instead of saying, "I don't like it when you're late," try, "I feel anxious when you're late. Can we agree to communicate better about our schedules?" This approach emphasizes your feelings and needs, making it easier for your partner to understand and respect your boundaries.

Respecting others' boundaries is just as important as setting your own. One effective strategy is to listen and actively acknowledge your partner's needs. When they express a boundary, show that you understand and are willing to honor it. This might involve adjusting your behavior to ensure that their boundaries are respected. For instance, if your partner needs personal space after a long day, give them that time to unwind without interruption. Recognizing and respecting these boundaries demonstrates empathy and consideration, strengthening your relationship.

Consider the story of David and Jaimie, a couple struggling to maintain personal space. David loved socializing, while Jamie needed quiet time to recharge. They decided to set clear boundaries around their personal space. David agreed to give Jaimie an hour of solitude each evening while Jaimie committed to participating in weekend social activities. This compromise made both partners feel respected and understood, improving their relationship.

Another example is Crystal and Ricky, who set boundaries to manage their work-life balance. They established specific times for work and family activities, ensuring that neither aspect overshadowed the other. This balance helped them maintain harmony and reduced stress in their relationship.

Role-Playing Scenarios for Real-Life Practice

Role-playing can be a transformative tool for improving relationship dynamics. It offers a safe space to practice and refine your communication skills without the pressure of real-life consequences. Imagine being able to rehearse difficult conversations, such as discussing finances or addressing a recurring conflict, in a controlled environment. This practice allows you to experiment with different approaches and receive immediate feedback, helping you build confidence and competence. The beauty of role-playing lies in its ability to simulate real-life scenarios, allowing you to practice assertive communication, conflict resolution, and boundary-setting in a supportive setting.

Consider a scenario for practicing assertive communication. You and your partner can take turns playing the roles of speaker and listener. The speaker might express a common concern, such as feeling overwhelmed by household responsibilities. Using "I" statements, the speaker can say, "I feel stressed when I have to manage all the chores by myself." The listener's role is to practice active listening, reflecting on what they heard and acknowledging the speaker's feelings. This exercise helps both partners become more comfortable expressing and receiving honest, assertive communication.

Another valuable scenario involves resolving a common relationship conflict. For instance, you could role-play a disagreement about spending habits. One partner might express concerns about overspending, while the other responds defensively. Through role-playing, you can practice staying calm and focused on finding a solution rather than escalating the conflict. This might involve brainstorming compromises, such as setting a monthly budget or agreeing to discuss major purchases beforehand. You can develop more effective real-life strategies for navigating conflicts by rehearsing these scenarios.

To set up an effective role-playing session, establish clear roles and objectives. Decide who will play the speaker and the listener, and outline the specific scenario you want to practice. Each partner should have a clear understanding of their role and the goals of the exercise. After completing the role-play, debrief and reflect on the experience. Discuss what worked well and what could be improved. This reflection helps you identify strengths and areas for growth, making future interactions more productive.

Consider the example of Randi and Kevin, who used role-playing to enhance communication. They practiced discussing their differing parenting styles, with Randi expressing her preference for structure and Kevin advocating for more flexibility. By role-playing this conversation, they explored each other's perspectives and found a balanced approach that worked for both. Another example is Olivia and Kelsey, who practiced boundary-setting through role-play. They simulated a scenario where Olivia needed alone time after work, and Kelsey learned to respect her boundaries without feeling neglected. This practice strengthened their relationship by fostering mutual understanding and respect.

Role-playing is a powerful tool for improving relationship dynamics, offering a safe space to practice and refine your skills. Simulating real-life scenarios allows you to build confidence and competence in communication, conflict resolution, and boundary-setting. This practice enhances your relationship with your partner and equips you with the tools to navigate life's challenges more effectively.

In the next chapter, we'll explore strategies for balancing professional and personal life and provide you with practical tools to manage both spheres without feeling overwhelmed.

SIX

Balancing Professional and Personal Life

Imagine you're at your office, surrounded by many tasks—emails demanding immediate attention, a report due by noon, and a thirty-minute meeting. The laundry pile is towering at home, and the kids need help with homework. It feels like you're juggling flaming torches, desperately trying not to drop any. This chaotic scene is all too familiar for many, but what if you could use some productivity hacks to streamline your day and bring a sense of calm to your life?

Productivity Hacks for Busy Women

Productivity hacks are strategies or tools designed to help you work smarter, not harder. They are especially valuable for busy women juggling multiple roles. These hacks are all about making small adjustments that significantly improve how you manage your time and tasks. By increasing your productivity, you can reduce stress and free up more time for the things that matter most to you, whether it's spending time with your family, pursuing a hobby, or simply relaxing.

One of the most effective productivity hacks is using project management apps like Trello or Asana. These tools allow you to organize your tasks visually, set deadlines, and track progress. Trello uses boards, lists, and cards to help you manage projects flexibly and intuitively. You can create a board for each project and use cards to represent tasks. Asana offers similar functionalities but with more robust features for team collaboration. Both tools help you track what needs to be done, who's responsible, and when it's due, reducing the mental load of remembering everything.

Time-tracking tools like Toggl can also be a game-changer. Toggl allows you to track how much time you spend on different tasks, providing insights into where your time goes. This awareness can help you identify areas where you might be wasting time and make adjustments to be more efficient. By understanding your time usage, you can better allocate your time to high-priority tasks and minimize distractions.

Practical tips can make a world of difference in improving productivity. The Pomodoro Technique is a popular method where you work in focused intervals of 25 minutes, followed by a 5-minute break. After four intervals, take a longer break. This technique helps maintain concentration and prevents burnout. Another helpful tool is the Eisenhower Matrix, which helps you prioritize tasks based on urgency and importance. By categorizing tasks into four quadrants—urgent and important, important but not urgent, urgent but not important, and neither urgent nor important—you can focus on what truly matters and delegate or eliminate the rest.

Consider the story of Emily, a marketing manager constantly overwhelmed by her workload. She started using time-blocking, a technique for allocating specific blocks of time for different tasks. Emily used Trello to organize her projects and set up her calendar with dedicated time for focused work, meetings, and breaks. This approach helped her stay organized and reduced her stress significantly.

Another example is Sarah, a working mother who felt like she was drowning in responsibilities at work and home. She began using Toggl to track her time and identify where she could be more efficient. Sarah also implemented the Pomodoro Technique during work hours and used the Eisenhower Matrix to prioritize her tasks. These small changes helped her balance her professional and personal life more effectively, giving her more time to spend with her family and lessening her anxiety.

Productivity hacks offer practical solutions to streamline your day, making managing professional and personal responsibilities easier. Incorporating these tools and techniques can enhance productivity, reduce stress, and create more time for what truly matters.

Delegation Techniques for the Workplace

Delegation involves assigning tasks to others, which reduces control behaviors and prevents burnout. By sharing responsibilities, you lighten your workload and allow others to contribute their skills and strengths. This not only helps you manage your time better but also fosters a sense of teamwork and collaboration. When you delegate, you free up mental space, reducing the pressure to handle everything yourself. This shift can improve mental health, increase productivity, and a more balanced life.

Effective delegation begins with identifying tasks suitable for others to handle. Start by listing all your responsibilities and pinpointing which ones can be delegated. Consider repetitive, time-consuming tasks or benefit from a fresh perspective. Once you've identified these tasks, choose team members with the skills and capacity to handle them. It's essential to communicate clearly when delegating. Provide detailed instructions, set clear expectations, and establish deadlines.

Open communication helps ensure that everyone understands their roles and responsibilities, reducing the risk of misunderstandings and errors.

One common barrier to delegation is the fear of losing control. You might worry that tasks won't be completed to your standards or that mistakes will reflect poorly on you. To overcome this, start small. Delegate minor tasks and gradually increase their complexity as you build trust in your team. Another challenge is ensuring accountability. It's crucial to follow up on delegated tasks without micromanaging. Set regular check-ins to review progress and provide support if needed. This approach helps maintain accountability while giving team members the autonomy to complete their tasks.

Consider the example of Jessica, a project manager who struggled with delegation for years. She felt projects would fall apart if she didn't oversee every detail. Realizing her limitations, she started delegating smaller tasks to her team. She communicated expectations and set regular check-ins. Over time, she saw her team thrive, bringing new ideas and efficiencies to the projects—this improved team dynamics and allowed Jessica to focus on strategic planning and leadership.

Another inspiring story is that of Monica, a professional balancing multiple projects at a tech company. She felt overwhelmed by the sheer volume of work and realized that delegation was her only way out. She began by identifying tasks that her team members could handle more efficiently. Monica communicated clearly, setting expectations and providing necessary resources. As she delegated more, she noticed a significant improvement in her workload management. Her team felt more empowered, and Monica had more time to focus on high-priority tasks, leading to better overall performance.

Delegation is a powerful tool for managing your workload and improving team dynamics. By sharing responsibilities and trusting your team, you can reduce stress, prevent burnout, and create a more balanced professional life.

Reducing Workplace Stress

Workplace stress can feel like a constant companion, especially when juggling numerous responsibilities. One of the most common sources of stress is a high workload coupled with tight deadlines. When you're constantly racing against the clock, it can feel overwhelming, leading to anxiety and burnout. Another significant stressor is the need for more control over work processes. You may have brilliant ideas and strategies, but rigid structures or micromanagement can stifle your creativity and make you feel powerless.

To combat these stressors, practicing mindfulness at work can be incredibly effective. Mindfulness involves being present in the moment and paying attention to your thoughts and emotions without judgment. Even a few minutes of mindfulness practice can help calm your mind and reduce stress. Setting realistic goals and expectations is another crucial strategy. Break down large projects into smaller, manageable tasks and set achievable deadlines. This makes the workload seem less daunting and provides a sense of accomplishment as you complete each task.

Managing work-related anxiety often requires actionable techniques. Taking regular breaks to recharge is essential. Stepping away from your desk, even for a short walk or a quick stretch, can help clear your mind and reduce stress levels. During particularly stressful moments, relaxation techniques like deep breathing can make a difference. Close your eyes, take a few deep breaths, and focus on breathing. This simple act can help you regain your composure and approach your tasks with a clearer mind.

Consider the story of Lisa, a project manager who felt overwhelmed by her demanding job. She began incorporating deep-breathing exercises into her workday, taking a few minutes each hour to breathe deeply and relax. This small change significantly impacted her stress levels, helping her stay calm and focused. Another example is Maria, an employee who struggled with the chaos of her work environment. She started organizing her tasks and setting realistic goals. By planning her day and breaking down her tasks, Maria reduced her stress and increased her productivity.

These strategies provide practical solutions to manage workplace stress effectively, allowing you to maintain your mental health and improve your work performance.

Creating a Work-Life Balance Plan

Balancing professional and personal life is more than a desirable goal; it's crucial for your overall well-being. When you achieve a balanced life, you can enjoy the benefits of reduced stress, improved mental health, and better physical health. A balanced life allows you to be more present in both your professional and personal spheres, enhancing your relationships and overall satisfaction. On the flip side, an imbalance can lead to burnout, chronic stress, and a host of health issues. It can also strain your relationships, making it harder to connect with loved ones and enjoy your life fully.

Creating a work-life balance plan begins with assessing your current situation. Take a moment to reflect on how you spend your time and identify areas where you need to be more relaxed. Are you spending too many hours at work? Is your personal life suffering as a result? Setting clear boundaries is the next step once you pinpoint the areas needing improvement. This might mean establishing specific work hours and sticking to them or setting aside dedicated time for family and self-care. Boundaries help create a structure that supports balance and prevents work from encroaching on personal time and vice versa.

Maintaining a balanced life requires ongoing effort and practical strategies. Scheduling regular downtime is crucial. Whether it's a weekly yoga class, a daily walk, or simply time spent reading a book, these moments of self-care help recharge your batteries and keep stress at bay. Communicating your boundaries with colleagues and family is equally important. Tell your team you won't be available after a certain hour, and inform your family about your work commitments. Clear communication ensures everyone is on the same page and respects your need for balance.

Consider the story of Anna, a software engineer who felt overwhelmed by her demanding job. She implemented a flexible work schedule that allowed her to work from home two days a week. This change gave her more time to spend with her young children and reduced her commute stress. She also set clear boundaries with her team, letting them know her availability and sticking to it. This plan not only improved her work performance but also enhanced her overall well-being.

Another example is Melissa, a marketing executive and mother of two. She prioritized family time through structured planning. She set aside an hour for family dinners every evening, followed by a no-work policy until the kids went to bed. She also scheduled regular date nights and solo weekend self-care activities with her partner. This structured approach helped Melissa balance her professional and personal responsibilities, leading to a more fulfilling and less stressful existence.

Managing Perfectionism at Work

Perfectionism in the workplace can be a double-edged sword. On one hand, it drives you to produce high-quality work. On the other, it can be a relentless taskmaster. Setting unrealistic standards often leads to burnout. You push yourself to the brink, striving for flawlessness in every project. This constant pressure can cause mental and physical exhaustion, making it difficult to sustain productivity over time.

The impact of perfectionism doesn't stop with you. It extends to your team and colleagues. You might expect the same from others when you hold yourself to impossibly high standards. This can create a tense work environment where no one feels good enough. Collaboration suffers because team members might shy away from contributing, fearing criticism or rejection. The stress of trying to meet these high expectations can stifle creativity and innovation, turning the workplace into a pressure cooker.

To manage perfectionism, start by setting realistic and achievable goals. Break larger projects into smaller, manageable tasks with clear, attainable objectives. This helps you stay focused and reduces the overwhelming feeling that everything must be perfect. Embrace the concept of "good enough." Understand that perfection isn't always necessary and that sometimes, good enough is perfectly acceptable. This mindset allows you to complete tasks more efficiently without getting bogged down by unnecessary details.

Adopting a growth mindset can also be a powerful way to combat perfectionism. Instead of seeing mistakes as failures, view them as learning opportunities. This shift in perspective encourages continuous improvement and reduces the fear of making errors. Focus on progress rather than perfection. Celebrate small victories and acknowledge the effort you put into your work, even if it's not flawless. This approach helps you build resilience and maintain a healthier work-life balance.

Take the example of Laura, a marketing director who struggled with perfectionism. She realized that her need for everything to be perfect was causing her immense stress and affecting her team. Laura began setting more realistic goals and embraced the "good enough" mindset. She also encouraged her team to share ideas without fear of criticism. This change fostered a more collaborative environment and improved overall productivity.

Another inspiring story is that of Teresa, an engineer who always aimed for perfection in her projects. This often led to delays and burnout. Teresa decided to focus on progress instead of perfection. She set achievable milestones and celebrated each one. This not only reduced her stress but also improved her performance. Her team noticed the positive change and followed her lead, creating a more supportive and productive work environment.

Relaxation Methods for Busy Schedules

Incorporating relaxation techniques into your daily routine is crucial for maintaining mental health, especially when juggling multiple roles and responsibilities. Regular relaxation helps to reduce stress, improve mood, and increase overall well-being. When you make time to relax, you're giving your mind and body a chance to reset, which can significantly reduce anxiety and the urge to control every detail of your life. This downtime isn't a luxury; it's necessary for anyone seeking balance and fulfillment.

The benefits of regular relaxation are numerous. It helps lower your heart rate and blood pressure, reduces muscle tension, and alleviates symptoms of anxiety and depression. When you take the time to relax, you also improve your focus and productivity, as a relaxed mind is better equipped to handle tasks efficiently. Moreover, incorporating relaxation into your routine can enhance your relationships by making you more present and less irritable.

Quick and easy relaxation techniques can be integrated into even the busiest schedules. A five-minute meditation session can work wonders. Find a quiet spot, close your eyes, and focus on your breath. Let your thoughts come and go without judgment. This brief practice can calm your mind and help you feel centered. Stretching exercises at your desk are another simple way to relax. Reach your arms above your head, roll your shoulders, and stretch your neck. These movements can relieve physical tension and refresh your mind.

Incorporating relaxation into your daily routine doesn't have to be complicated. Schedule short relaxation breaks throughout your day. Set a timer to remind yourself to take a five-minute break every hour. Use this time to stretch, breathe deeply, or simply close your eyes and relax. Creating a calming evening routine can also make a significant difference. Dim the lights, play soft music, and engage in activities that help you unwind, such as reading a book or taking a warm bath. This routine signals your body that it's time to relax and prepare for restful sleep.

Consider Emily, a busy lawyer who felt constantly on edge. She started incorporating short meditation sessions during her work breaks. Five minutes of focused breathing helped her manage stress and improve her concentration. Another example is Lisa, a working mother of two. She introduced her children to simple relaxation techniques like deep breathing and gentle stretching before bedtime. This practice helped her relax and created a calming routine for her kids, improving their sleep and overall mood.

Integrating relaxation methods into your busy schedule is a practical way to reduce stress and improve well-being. These techniques are simple yet effective, making it easier to navigate the demands of daily life with a calm and balanced mind.

Balancing professional and personal life requires a combination of effective strategies and practical tools. You can achieve a more fulfilling and less stressful life by incorporating relaxation methods, managing perfectionism, and creating a work-life balance plan. In the next chapter, we'll explore how to build a support network to enhance your well-being further.

SEVEN

Managing Technology and Digital Distractions

Envision you're at your desk, intending to finish that important report before lunch. Your phone buzzes with a notification—another email or a social media alert. You glance at it, thinking it'll just take a second, but soon, you find yourself scrolling through your feed, watching cute cat videos, and reading articles you didn't plan on. Before you know it, an hour has slipped by, and you're left feeling guilty and more stressed than before. While incredibly useful, technology can be a double-edged sword, especially when managing control behaviors.

Impact of Technology on Control Behaviors

Technology has become integral to our lives, weaving into nearly every aspect of our daily routines. From smartphones and laptops to smart home devices, technology provides convenience and efficiency. However, it also has a significant impact on our control behaviors. On one hand, technology can exacerbate the need for control. The constant flow of information and the pressure to stay connected can create a sense of urgency and anxiety. You might feel compelled to check your emails every few minutes or respond to every notification immediately, believing that staying on top of things will help you maintain control. This constant connectivity can lead to hypervigilance, where you're always on alert, ready to react to the next digital disruption.

On the other hand, technology can also be a powerful tool for managing control behaviors. Various apps and tools are designed to help you organize your tasks, set reminders, and manage your time effectively. For instance, project management apps like Trello and Asana allow you to visualize your tasks, set deadlines, and track your progress. These tools can help you plan and execute your responsibilities without feeling overwhelmed. Additionally, digital calendars like Google Calendar can help you schedule your day, set reminders, and allocate time for breaks and self-care. Using technology mindfully, you can create a sense of structure and order, reducing the need to control every detail manually.

However, the effects of constant connectivity and digital distractions on mental health cannot be ignored. The barrage of notifications, emails, and social media updates can create a constant distraction, making it difficult to focus on tasks and decreasing productivity. This can exacerbate feelings of anxiety and stress as you struggle to manage your responsibilities amidst the digital noise. The fear of missing out (FOMO) can further fuel this anxiety, making you feel compelled to stay connected and up-to-date with everything happening around you. This constant state of alertness can take a toll on your mental health, leading to burnout and emotional exhaustion.

Consider the story of Emma, a marketing executive constantly overwhelmed by work and personal responsibilities. She always kept her phone by her side, checking emails and messages even during family dinners. This constant connectivity made her feel stressed and anxious as she struggled to balance her work and personal life. Realizing the impact on her mental health, Emma decided to make some changes. She set specific times during the day to check her emails and turned off non-essential notifications. She also used a digital calendar to schedule her tasks and allocate time for breaks. These small adjustments helped her regain control without feeling overwhelmed by technology.

Another example is Sarah, a mother of two who struggled with the pressure to stay connected through social media. She constantly compared her life to others, feeling inadequate and stressed. To address this, Sarah decided to take a digital detox, limiting her social media usage to specific times of the day. She also unfollowed accounts that triggered negative feelings and started following pages that promoted positivity and self-care. This mindful approach to technology helped Sarah reduce her anxiety and focus on what truly mattered in her life.

While technology can contribute to control behaviors, it can also be leveraged as a tool for better management. The key is to use it mindfully and purposefully, setting boundaries and creating a balance that works for you. By understanding the impact of technology on your mental health and control behaviors, you can make informed choices that enhance your well-being and productivity.

Reflection Exercise: Assess Your Technology Habits

Take a moment to reflect on your relationship with technology. Consider the following questions:

1. How often do you check your phone or email during the day?
2. Do you feel anxious or stressed when you're not connected or up-to-date with notifications?
3. How does constant connectivity affect your productivity and mental health?

4. Are there specific apps or tools that help you manage your tasks and responsibilities effectively?
5. What changes can you make to use technology more mindfully and reduce digital distractions?

Write down your thoughts and observations in a journal. Identifying your habits and their impact on your life is the first step towards making positive changes. Remember, the goal is to create a balanced and mindful approach to technology that supports your well-being and helps you manage control behaviors effectively.

Technology can be a source of stress and a tool for better management. By understanding its impact on your control behaviors and mental health, you can make informed choices that enhance your well-being and productivity. Use technology mindfully, set boundaries, and create a balance that works for you. This approach will help you reclaim control without feeling overwhelmed by the digital world.

Strategies for Healthy Technology Use

You know that feeling when you've spent hours scrolling through social media or answering emails and suddenly realize the whole evening has slipped away? It's easy to let technology take over our lives without even noticing. The key to healthy technology use lies in setting boundaries. One effective way to do this is by establishing screen time limits. For instance, you might decide that after 8 PM, your phone goes on "Do Not Disturb" mode. This simple boundary can free up your evenings for activities that enrich your life, like spending quality time with family or diving into a good book.

Digital detoxes are another powerful tool. These are periods when you intentionally disconnect from all digital devices. It might be a full day over the weekend or just a few hours each evening. The goal is to create a space where you can recharge without the constant buzz of notifications. During a digital detox, you could engage in activities that ground you—like taking a walk, cooking a meal from scratch, or engaging in a hobby. It's about finding joy and relaxation in the real world, away from screens. Think of it as a mini-vacation for your mind.

Mindful and purposeful use of technology is essential for maintaining a healthy relationship with your devices. Start by being intentional about when and why you're using technology. Before opening an app or checking your phone, ask yourself if it's necessary. Are you reaching for your phone out of habit or boredom? If so, consider what else you could do that would be more fulfilling. Set specific times for checking emails and social media rather than constantly being available. This helps you stay focused and reduces the anxiety of being perpetually connected.

Creating designated tech-free zones in your home can also help. For example, make the dining room where phones are not allowed. This encourages meaningful conversations during meals and fosters a stronger connection with your loved ones. The bedroom is another great tech-free zone. Removing electronic devices from your sleeping area can improve the quality of your sleep and make your bedroom a sanctuary for rest. Invest in an old-fashioned alarm clock to wake you up instead of relying on your phone, which can tempt you to check messages and notifications first thing in the morning.

Another strategy is to customize your notifications. Not all notifications are created equal; some are more disruptive than others. Go through your phone settings and disable non-essential notifications. Do you need to know every time someone likes your photo or comments on a post? Limiting notifications to only the most important ones can significantly reduce digital distractions. This helps you stay focused on the task and reduces the urge to check your phone constantly.

Being mindful about the content you consume is equally important. Curate your social media feeds to include accounts that inspire and uplift you. Unfollow or mute pages that trigger stress, anxiety, or negative feelings. Social media should be a source of joy and connection, not a breeding ground for comparison and self-doubt. Follow pages that align with your interests and values, and engage with content that enriches your life. This simple act of curating your feed can transform your social media experience from draining to empowering.

Consider implementing tech-free times in your daily routine. For instance, try starting your day without immediately reaching for your phone. Instead, spend the first 30 minutes doing something that sets a positive tone for the day, like stretching, meditating, or journaling. The same goes for the end of the day. Power down your devices at least an hour before bed and engage in calming activities that help you wind down. This can improve your sleep quality and overall mental well-being.

Another helpful practice is the "one-screen rule." This means using only one screen at a time. If you're watching a movie, put your phone away. If you're working on your computer, close unnecessary tabs and avoid checking your phone. This not only helps you stay focused but also allows you to immerse yourself fully in the activity at hand. It's about being present and mindful rather than letting technology simultaneously pull you in multiple directions.

To make these strategies more effective, involve your family or household members. Create a family tech plan where everyone agrees on specific rules and boundaries around technology use. This could include tech-free family dinners, weekend digital detoxes, or setting screen time limits for children. By involving everyone, you create a supportive environment that makes it easier to stick to these boundaries and encourages healthier technology habits for the entire family.

Let's not forget about the importance of regular breaks. The Pomodoro Technique, which involves working for 25 minutes and then taking a 5-minute break, can be incredibly effective. Use these breaks to step away from screens and do something refreshing, like stretching, grabbing a glass of water, or simply looking out the window. These short breaks can prevent burnout and keep your mind sharp, making you more productive and focused.

Lastly, consider the benefits of analog activities. Sometimes, the best way to reduce screen time is to replace it with something equally engaging but non-digital. Pick up a new hobby like crocheting, painting, or gardening. Read a physical book instead of an e-book. Write in a journal instead of typing on a computer. These activities can be incredibly fulfilling and provide a much-needed break from the constant stimulation of digital devices.

Balancing Technology and Real-Life Interactions

Think about the last time you were out with friends and noticed that everyone, including yourself, was more engaged with their phones than with each other. It's a common scene where digital interactions overshadow face-to-face conversations, neglecting real-life connections. In today's world, balancing technology and real-life interactions is more important than ever. While technology offers countless benefits, it can also disrupt meaningful relationships if not managed carefully.

Human interactions are the cornerstone of emotional well-being. When you connect with someone face-to-face, you engage in a rich exchange of verbal and non-verbal cues that simply can't be replicated through a screen. Eye contact, body language, and even the tone of voice contribute to a deeper understanding and emotional connection. These interactions help build trust, empathy, and a sense of belonging, all crucial for mental health. When technology takes precedence over these real-life moments, it can create a sense of isolation and disconnection. You might feel lonely even when you're "connected" to hundreds of people online.

It's also worth noting that real-life interactions offer an opportunity for spontaneous and genuine moments that digital communication often lacks. Think about the joy of a surprise visit from a friend or the shared laughter over an unexpected joke during a conversation. These moments enrich our lives and contribute to our overall happiness. When constantly distracted by your phone or other devices, you miss out on these priceless experiences. Balancing technology with real-life interactions means being present at the moment and fully engaging with the people around you.

Creating tech-free zones and times in your daily routine can be a game-changer. For instance, designate the dining table as a no-phone zone. This simple rule encourages everyone to engage in meaningful conversations during meals. You might learn more about your partner's day, your children's thoughts, or your friends' experiences. These conversations can strengthen your relationships and provide a sense of connection that no amount of digital interaction can replace. Similarly, consider setting aside specific times in the day when you put away your devices. Whether during your morning coffee, evening walk, or bedtime routine, these tech-free moments allow you to focus on yourself and the people around you.

Remember the importance of engaging in activities that limit your screen time while fostering real-life connections. Joining a local club, attending community events, or participating in group activities like sports or book clubs can help you build new relationships and strengthen existing ones. These activities offer a break from the digital world and provide opportunities for face-to-face interactions. They also allow you to pursue interests and hobbies that bring joy and fulfillment, contributing to a balanced and enriching life.

Consider the impact of technology on family dynamics. Children, in particular, are highly influenced by the behavior of adults around them. If they see you constantly glued to your phone, they will likely mimic that behavior. Setting a good example by balancing your screen time can encourage healthier habits in your children. Engage in family activities that don't involve screens, like board games, outdoor adventures, or cooking together. These activities strengthen family bonds and create lasting memories that digital interactions can't offer.

Balancing technology with real-life interactions can enhance your work relationships and overall job satisfaction. While emails and instant messages are convenient, they can't replace the value of face-to-face meetings and discussions. Opt for in-person meetings or video calls that allow for more personal interaction whenever possible. These conversations can lead to better understanding, increased collaboration, and stronger professional relationships. They also enable spontaneous brainstorming and problem-solving, which can be more challenging through digital communication.

One practical approach to balancing technology and real-life interactions is being intentional about digital consumption. Before reaching for your phone or opening a social media app, ask yourself if it's necessary or if there's a more fulfilling activity you could engage in. This mindfulness can help you make more conscious choices about your time. It can also reduce the feeling of being overwhelmed by digital distractions, allowing you to focus on what truly matters.

Another strategy is to use technology to enhance rather than replace real-life interactions. For example, use social media to plan and organize get-togethers with friends or family. Share photos and updates to stay connected, but don't let it substitute for face-to-face interactions. Technology can be a great tool for maintaining relationships, but there are other ways to connect with others. Prioritize in-person meetings and experiences whenever possible, and use digital tools as a supplement rather than a replacement.

Balancing technology and real-life interactions is crucial for maintaining healthy relationships, reducing stress, and enhancing overall well-being. You can create a more balanced and fulfilling life by being mindful of your digital consumption, creating tech-free zones and times, and prioritizing face-to-face interactions. Remember, the goal is not to eliminate technology but to use it to support and enhance your real-life connections.

As we move forward, we'll explore how to build a support network to enhance your well-being further and help you navigate the challenges of balancing your professional and personal life.

EIGHT

Parenting Without Control

Picture for a moment that you're at the park, watching your child play on the swings. You notice another parent hovering closely, directing every move their child makes. They try to ensure everything goes perfectly, but the child's frustration grows. This scene is all too common, underscoring the importance of setting healthy boundaries. As parents, the urge to control every aspect of our children's lives can be strong, but stepping back and allowing them to grow independently is crucial.

Setting Healthy Boundaries with Children

Establishing boundaries with your children is essential for fostering respect and understanding in your relationship. Boundaries help children learn what is acceptable and what isn't, promoting a sense of security and stability. They also teach children self-discipline, a vital skill for navigating the complexities of life. When boundaries are clear and consistently enforced, children understand the expectations and feel more confident in their actions.

Let's discuss how to establish these boundaries. Start by setting age-appropriate limits. This might mean simple rules for younger children, like putting toys away after playtime. For teenagers, boundaries could include curfews and guidelines for social media use. The key is ensuring these boundaries are relevant to their developmental stage and capabilities.

Consistency is crucial when it comes to enforcing rules. If a boundary is set, it must be upheld each time the situation arises. Inconsistency can confuse children and undermine the boundary's effectiveness. For example, if screen time is limited to one hour daily, this rule should be consistently applied. Exceptions can be made for special occasions, but they should be communicated and understood as rare.

Communicating boundaries effectively is just as important as setting them. Use positive language when explaining rules to your children. Instead of saying, "Don't leave your toys out," try, "Please put your toys away when you're done playing." Positive language focuses on desired behaviors rather than prohibiting actions, making it easier for children to understand and follow the rules.

Involving your children in setting these boundaries can also be beneficial. When children participate in creating rules, they are more likely to understand and respect them. For instance, if you're setting limits on screen time, discuss with your child what they think is a reasonable amount and why. This collaborative approach fosters a sense of ownership and responsibility.

Here are some specific examples of healthy boundaries. Setting screen time limits can prevent overuse and promote a balanced lifestyle. For instance, you might allow one hour of screen time on weekdays and two hours on weekends. Bedtime routines are another area where boundaries are essential. A consistent bedtime helps children get the rest they need and creates a sense of predictability. You might set a rule that lights go out at 8 PM, with a calming bedtime routine leading up to it.

Reflect and Implement

Take a moment to consider the boundaries you currently have for your children. Are they age-appropriate and consistently enforced? Reflect on how you communicate these rules and how your children respond. Make a list of any areas where boundaries could be improved or added. Discuss these with your children and involve them in setting new limits.

The next section will explore how encouraging independence can further support your child's growth and development.

Encouraging Independence in Kids

Encouraging independence in your children is one of the most empowering gifts you can offer them. It builds self-confidence and teaches them invaluable problem-solving skills. When children learn to navigate challenges independently, they develop a sense of capability and resilience. Independence also fosters a sense of responsibility, helping them understand the consequences of their actions and decisions.

One effective strategy for encouraging autonomy is allowing your children to make choices. Start with simple decisions, such as choosing their clothes for the day or selecting a healthy snack. As they age, you can expand their choices to more significant decisions, like planning a family outing or managing their allowance. This empowers them and teaches them the importance of making thoughtful decisions.

Encouraging self-help skills is another crucial aspect. Teach your children to manage basic tasks independently, like tying their shoes, packing their school bags, or preparing a simple meal. These small steps build their confidence and competence, showing them they can care for themselves. It's essential to offer guidance initially but gradually step back as they become more proficient. This balance between support and freedom is key to fostering independence without overwhelming them.

Knowing when to step back is an art in itself. It's natural to want to step in and help when you see your child struggling, but sometimes, letting them work through challenges independently is more beneficial. This doesn't mean abandoning them; instead, it's about offering support without taking over. For example, if your child is working on a homework assignment, resist the urge to correct every mistake immediately. Instead, provide guidance and encourage them to find solutions independently when asked.

Real-life examples can illustrate how powerful these strategies can be. Take the story of Olivia, a five-year-old who loves picking out her clothes each morning. Her parents noticed that allowing her this choice made her more excited about getting dressed and ready for school. It also reduced morning conflicts, as Olivia felt more in control of her routine. Then there's Sam, a ten-year-old who manages his homework schedule. His parents gave him the responsibility of deciding when to do his assignments, with the understanding that all work must be completed by bedtime. Sam learned to prioritize tasks and manage his time effectively, which will benefit him in the long run.

Encouraging independence is about striking a balance. It's about providing the right amount of guidance while allowing your child the freedom to explore and learn from their experiences. This balance helps them grow into confident, capable individuals who trust their abilities and judgment. By fostering independence, you're not just preparing them for the challenges of today but also equipping them for the uncertainties of tomorrow.

Positive Reinforcement Techniques

Positive reinforcement is a powerful parenting tool that rewards desirable behaviors and encourages repetition. Unlike punishment, which aims to stop unwanted actions, positive reinforcement strengthens good behavior by providing a motivational boost. At its core, positive reinforcement involves adding a pleasant consequence immediately after a behavior occurs, making the behavior more likely to be repeated. This approach improves behavior and boosts children's self-esteem and confidence, fostering a more positive and nurturing environment.

One effective method for using positive reinforcement is praising effort and progress rather than just outcomes. For example, if your child spends time studying for a test, praise their dedication and hard work, regardless of the final grade. This reinforcement emphasizes the value of effort and perseverance, teaching children that the process is just as important as the result. It helps them understand that their hard work is noticed and appreciated, motivating them to continue putting in effort.

Using reward systems can also be an effective way to reinforce positive behavior. Create a simple chart where your child can earn stickers or points for completing tasks or displaying good behavior. Once they accumulate certain stickers or points, they can trade them in for a reward, such as extra playtime or a special outing. This system provides a clear and tangible way for children to see the benefits of their positive actions, making it more likely that they will continue to behave well.

However, it's crucial to avoid common pitfalls when using positive reinforcement. Over-reliance on material rewards can backfire, as children may start to expect a tangible reward for every good deed, diminishing intrinsic motivation. To counter this, mix material rewards with non-material ones, such as verbal praise, extra playtime, or a special activity. Inconsistent application is another common mistake. If you only occasionally reinforce positive behavior, the effectiveness of the reinforcement diminishes. Ensure that you consistently acknowledge and reward desirable behaviors to maintain their impact.

Consider the story of Ava, who used positive reinforcement to encourage her son to complete his chores. Instead of simply telling him to clean his room, she praised his efforts each time he made progress, no matter how small. Over time, her son began to take pride in his tidy space and needed less prompting to keep it clean. Similarly, Lisa used a reward system to encourage her daughter to practice the piano regularly. By earning points for each practice session, her daughter felt motivated and looked forward to her practice time, leading to noticeable improvement in her skills.

Positive reinforcement can be a game-changer in parenting. It encourages desirable behavior and fosters a supportive and positive environment where children feel valued and motivated. By praising effort, using reward systems wisely, and avoiding common pitfalls, you can effectively harness the power of positive reinforcement to enhance your child's development and create a happier, more harmonious home.

Creating a Nurturing Home Environment

Creating a nurturing home environment is more than just providing physical comfort; it fosters emotional safety and support. A nurturing home is where everyone feels valued, loved, and encouraged. It's a place where children can express themselves without fear of judgment, knowing they have a safe space to return to no matter what. Emotional safety means children feel secure enough to share their feelings and thoughts openly. Support means being there for them, offering guidance and encouragement, and celebrating their successes while helping them navigate their failures.

To cultivate such an environment, start by establishing family rituals. These rituals, whether as simple as a weekly movie night or as elaborate as holiday traditions, create a sense of belonging and stability. They offer regular opportunities for family members to connect and bond. For instance, having Sunday dinners where everyone shares their weekly highs and lows can foster open communication and strengthen family ties.

Another crucial step is creating a positive and open communication culture. Encourage family members to discuss their feelings and experiences without fear of criticism. Use active listening to show that you value their perspectives. This means paying attention when someone speaks, asking questions, and reflecting on what you've heard. Open communication helps build trust and ensures that everyone feels heard and understood.

Balancing structure and flexibility in the home is essential for maintaining a nurturing environment. While routines provide a sense of order and predictability, leaving room for spontaneity and adaptability is important. Set routines that include necessary activities like homework and chores and allow for unplanned fun and relaxation. Being adaptable to changes, such as a spontaneous family outing or an impromptu dance party in the living room, can make home life more enjoyable and less rigid.

Consider the story of the Johnson family, who hold regular family meetings every Sunday evening. During these meetings, each family member can speak about their week, voice any concerns, and suggest activities for the upcoming week. This practice keeps everyone informed and makes everyone feel valued and involved in family decisions. Another example is the Smith household, which focuses on emotional well-being. They've created a "calm corner" in their home, filled with comfy cushions, books, and calming activities like coloring and puzzles. Anyone overwhelmed can retreat to this corner to relax and regain their composure.

These real-life examples illustrate that a nurturing home environment is built on emotional safety, support, and open communication. Establishing family rituals and balancing structure with flexibility can transform your home into a sanctuary where every member feels cherished and understood.

Handling Parenting Stress

Parenting is a beautiful yet challenging role that often feels like a constant juggling act. On any given day, you might find yourself balancing work deadlines with school pickups, meal planning with homework help, and still trying to carve out a moment. The stress from juggling these multiple roles can be overwhelming. Society's high expectations only add to the pressure, making you feel like you must excel at everything. This constant strain can lead to burnout, affecting you and your entire family.

To manage this stress, it's crucial to practice self-care and mindfulness. Self-care isn't selfish; it's essential. Take time each day, even if it's just a few minutes, to do something that rejuvenates you. Whether reading a book, taking a walk, or simply sitting quietly with a cup of tea, these moments can help recharge your mental and emotional batteries. Mindfulness practices, such as deep breathing exercises or short meditation sessions, can also be incredibly effective. They help ground you in the present moment, reducing anxiety and helping you approach challenges with a clearer mind.

Seeking support from friends and family can make a world of difference. Don't hesitate to lean on your support network. Share your struggles with a trusted friend or family member; discussing your stress can sometimes alleviate some of the burden. If your stress levels are unmanageable, consider joining a parenting support group. These groups offer a safe space to share experiences and gain insights from others in similar situations. Sometimes, just knowing you're not alone can provide immense relief.

Open communication is another vital aspect of managing parenting stress. Talk to your partner about your stressors and work together to find solutions. Both of you must be on the same page and support each other. Recognize the signs of burnout, such as constant fatigue, irritability, or a sense of detachment, and take action before it worsens. Seek professional help if needed, whether it's through counseling or stress management workshops. Addressing these issues early can prevent them from escalating into more serious problems.

Consider the story of Rebecca, a mother of two who felt overwhelmed by her daily responsibilities. She started practicing mindfulness techniques, such as deep breathing and short meditation, in the mornings before the kids woke up. This simple practice helped her start the day with a sense of calm and focus. Another example is Maria, who joined a local parenting group after feeling isolated and stressed. The support and camaraderie she found there significantly improved her ability to manage stress and find joy in parenting again.

Incorporating these stress-management techniques can transform your daily life. By taking care of yourself, seeking support, and communicating openly, you can handle parenting challenges more effectively and create a healthier, happier environment for your family.

Building Trust with Your Children

Building trust with your children is the cornerstone of a healthy parent-child relationship. Trust forms the foundation for open communication, making it easier for them to come to you with their concerns, joys, and questions. When your child trusts you, they feel secure and confident, knowing they have a safe space to express themselves without fear of judgment. This sense of security is crucial for their emotional development and overall well-being.

Consistency and reliability are key to fostering trust. Children need to know they can count on you to be there when you say you will be. This means following through on promises and being dependable. If you promise to attend their soccer game or help with homework, ensure you do. Consistency in your actions builds a solid foundation of trust over time.

Showing empathy and understanding is another powerful way to build trust. When your child shares their feelings or experiences, listen actively and validate their emotions. Avoid dismissing their concerns, no matter how minor they may seem. Instead, acknowledge their feelings and show that you understand. Phrases like, "I can see that you're upset about this," or "It sounds like that was tough for you," can go a long way in making your child feel heard and understood.

Maintaining trust requires ongoing effort and attention. Keep your promises, no matter how small they may seem. Follow through if you promise a trip to the park on the weekend. Breaking promises can erode trust and make your child reluctant to rely on you in the future. Being present and attentive is equally important. Put away distractions, like your phone or work, and give your child full attention when needed. This shows them that they are your priority and that you value your time together.

Consider the story of Jenna, who promised her daughter a special outing to the zoo on Saturday. Despite a busy week, Jenna kept her promise, and the two had a wonderful day. Following through on a commitment strengthened their bond and reinforced Jenna's reliability in her daughter's eyes. Another example is the Goldstein family, who engage in trust-building games and activities. Every Friday, they have a family game night where everyone gets to choose a game. These activities not only build trust but also foster a sense of teamwork and fun.

Building trust with your children is an ongoing process that requires consistency, empathy, and presence. You can create a strong, trusting relationship that provides a solid foundation for your child's growth and development by being reliable, showing understanding, and maintaining your commitments.

In the next chapter, we'll explore how to navigate societal and cultural pressures, helping you and your family find a path that's true to yourselves amidst external expectations.

NINE

Navigating Societal and Cultural Pressures

See yourself at a family gathering, and the conversation turns to your career and personal life. Relatives offer unsolicited advice, subtly hinting that you should focus more on family or implying that your career ambitions are too lofty. You smile politely, but inside, it's a struggle. The pressure to conform to traditional roles is palpable, a challenge many women face daily.

Breaking Free from Traditional Roles

Societal and cultural expectations have long shaped traditional gender roles, influencing how women perceive their roles in both personal and professional spheres. Historically, gender roles have been deeply ingrained, guiding how men and women should behave, think, and interact. Women were often expected to prioritize family and caregiving over personal ambitions. These roles were passed down through generations, creating a framework many still feel compelled to follow. The pressure to conform to these norms can be overwhelming, leading to a constant struggle between fulfilling societal expectations and pursuing personal desires.

These traditional roles often limit personal growth and fulfillment. Internalized expectations can stifle your ambitions and passions, making you feel that certain paths are off-limits. For instance, you might shy away from pursuing a demanding career because it doesn't align with the traditional primary caregiver role. This internal conflict can create a sense of dissatisfaction and unfulfillment as you suppress your true aspirations to fit into a predefined mold. The effect on career choices and personal aspirations can be significant, leading to missed opportunities and unrealized potential.

Breaking free from these traditional roles involves challenging the status quo and setting personal goals independent of societal expectations. Start by reflecting on what you truly want without the influence of external pressures. Write down your goals and aspirations, focusing on what brings you joy and fulfillment. Seek support from like-minded communities where you can share experiences and find encouragement. Surrounding yourself with individuals who understand and support your journey can be empowering and validating.

Consider the story of Mia, who pursued a non-traditional career in engineering. Growing up, she faced constant pressure to choose a more "suitable" profession for women, like teaching or nursing. Despite this, Mia followed her passion for technology and engineering. She faced numerous challenges, including skepticism from family and peers. However, her determination and support from a network of like-minded women in STEM helped her succeed. Today, Mia is a successful engineer, breaking barriers and inspiring other women to pursue their passions.

Another example is Megan, a mother who found a way to balance her career and family life without guilt. Megan felt immense pressure to either focus solely on her career or be a stay-at-home mom. She created her path, setting boundaries and prioritizing tasks aligned with her values. Megan sought flexible work arrangements and involved her family in household responsibilities. This approach allowed her to thrive professionally and personally, showing that balancing multiple roles is possible without succumbing to societal pressures.

Breaking free from traditional roles requires courage and determination, but the rewards are immense. You can create a fulfilling life that aligns with your true self by setting personal goals, seeking support, and challenging societal norms.

Finding Your Path

Imagine sitting at a cozy café, sipping your favorite drink, and daydreaming about what truly excites you. This moment of self-discovery is where finding your path begins. It's about peeling back the layers of societal expectations and focusing on what genuinely ignites your passion. Exploring personal interests and passions is crucial. Think about activities that make you lose track of time. Whether painting, coding, gardening, or writing, these interests often hold the key to your true path. Assessing your strengths and values can further guide you. Reflect on what you're naturally good at and what principles you hold dear. These insights can help shape a life that feels true to you.

Setting personal goals aligned with your values is the next step. This isn't just about career aspirations but about creating a life that resonates with your inner self. Start by creating a vision board. Gather images, quotes, and symbols that represent your dreams and goals. Place it somewhere you can see daily as a visual reminder of what you're working towards. Writing a personal mission statement can also be empowering. This statement should encapsulate what you stand for and aim to achieve. It is a guiding star, helping you stay focused on your path even when obstacles arise.

Obstacles are inevitable, but overcoming them is part of the journey. Dealing with self-doubt and fear is a common challenge. When those negative thoughts creep in, remind yourself of your strengths and achievements. Building resilience and perseverance is essential. Consider setbacks as learning opportunities rather than failures. Surround yourself with supportive people who encourage you to keep going, even when the going gets tough.

Take the story of Sidney, a corporate lawyer who realized her true passion lay in the culinary arts. Despite the stability and prestige of her legal career, she felt unfulfilled. Sidney took a leap of faith, enrolled in culinary school, and eventually opened her own restaurant. Her journey was fraught with challenges, including peer skepticism and financial hurdles. However, her unwavering passion and resilience led her to success, and she now enjoys a fulfilling career that aligns with her true self.

Another inspiring example is Lily, who always dreamed of traveling the world and writing about her experiences. Stuck in a monotonous 9-to-5 job, she felt her dreams slipping away. Determined to change her life, Lily started a travel blog on weekends. It gained traction, and she eventually transitioned to full-time travel writing. Despite societal pressures to maintain a "stable" job, Lily followed her passion and created a life that brought her joy and fulfillment.

Finding your path is about embracing what makes you unique and pursuing it with tenacity. By focusing on self-discovery, setting aligned goals, and overcoming obstacles, you can create a life that reflects your identity.

Handling Societal Expectations

Societal expectations can feel like an invisible weight pressing down on you, dictating how you should act, look, and even think. These expectations often set an impossibly high bar, especially for women.

You're expected to excel in every role you play—whether it's as a mother, employee, partner, or friend. This constant pressure to be perfect can lead to stress and control behaviors. You might be micromanaging every detail of your life, believing it's the only way to meet these high standards. Media and cultural influences play a significant role in shaping these expectations. From glossy magazine covers showcasing flawless mothers to social media feeds filled with curated perfection, it's easy to feel you're falling short. These images and narratives reinforce the idea that you must always have it together.

Setting personal boundaries is crucial to manage these expectations without succumbing to them. This means learning to say no when demands become overwhelming and prioritizing tasks that align with your values. For instance, if you're asked to take on additional work at your job but it interferes with your family time, it's okay to decline. Prioritizing self-care and mental health is also essential. Make time for activities that rejuvenate you, whether reading a book, walking, or practicing yoga. These moments of self-care can help you recharge and maintain your emotional well-being.

Critical thinking is another powerful tool in navigating societal expectations. It's about questioning cultural narratives and making choices based on values rather than societal norms. Ask yourself why you feel compelled to meet certain expectations. Are they aligned with your values, or do external pressures impose them? Making informed choices means being true to yourself and not just following the crowd. This critical evaluation helps you break free from the cycle of control and anxiety that societal expectations can create.

Consider the story of Shari, a mother who rejected the "supermom" stereotype. She felt immense pressure to excel at work, maintain a spotless home, and be constantly available for her children. This unrealistic standard left her exhausted and stressed. Shari decided to set boundaries and prioritize her well-being. She involved her family in household chores, set realistic expectations at work, and made time for self-care. This shift allowed her to find balance and reduce the need for control.

Another example is Kate, a professional who learned to set boundaries to maintain a work-life balance. She faced constant pressure to be available 24/7, leading to burnout. Kate began to set clear boundaries with her employer and colleagues, specifying her work hours and unplugging after office hours. This change improved her mental health and made her more productive and focused during work hours. You can navigate these pressures by managing societal expectations through boundaries, self-care, and critical thinking without losing yourself.

Embracing Your Authentic Self

Authenticity is about being true to yourself and embracing yourself without pretense or fear of judgment. It's about aligning your actions and words with your true beliefs and values. Living authentically means not hiding behind societal masks or trying to fit into boxes that don't suit you. Instead, you're confidently showing up as yourself, with all your unique quirks and traits. Authenticity allows you to live a genuine and fulfilling life, free from the constraints of trying to be something you're not.

Characteristics of authenticity include self-awareness, honesty, and vulnerability. Self-awareness involves understanding your strengths, weaknesses, and true desires. Honesty means being truthful with yourself and others, even when uncomfortable. Vulnerability, though often seen as a weakness, is a strength. It involves embracing your imperfections and being open about your struggles. These traits form the foundation of an authentic life, allowing you to connect deeply with yourself and others.

Living authentically brings numerous benefits. It leads to greater self-confidence because you are no longer trying to be someone you're not. You also experience deeper and more meaningful relationships, as authenticity fosters trust and mutual respect. Additionally, being true to yourself reduces stress and anxiety. You're not constantly worrying about meeting others' expectations or maintaining a facade. Instead, you can relax and enjoy life, knowing that you are living in alignment with your true self.

Embracing your authentic self requires self-acceptance. Start by practicing self-compassion. Treat yourself with the same kindness and understanding that you would offer a friend. When you make mistakes, acknowledge them without harsh self-criticism. Understand that everyone has flaws and that these imperfections make you human. Embracing your vulnerabilities means acknowledging your fears and struggles without shame. It's about understanding that vulnerability is a powerful tool for connection and growth.

Authenticity is crucial in relationships. Communicate openly and honestly with your partner, friends, and family. Share your thoughts, feelings, and desires without fear of judgment. Building connections based on mutual respect means valuing each other's authenticity. Encourage your loved ones to be themselves and appreciate them for who they are. This creates a supportive and nurturing environment where everyone feels valued and understood.

Consider the story of Maria, who embraced her unique identity in her career. She always felt pressured to conform to corporate expectations, hiding her creative side. One day, she incorporated her passion for art into her work. She started leading creative workshops at her company, which brought her joy and improved team dynamics. Her authenticity inspired others to embrace their passions, creating a more innovative and fulfilling workplace.

Another example is Jessica, a mother who fostered authenticity in her family. She encouraged open communication and allowed her children to express their true selves, creating a home environment where everyone felt safe and valued. Jessica's authenticity in her parenting fostered trust and deep connections with her children, creating a supportive and loving family dynamic.

Stories of Women Who Overcame Control Issues

Inspiration often comes from real-life stories, and many women have successfully navigated the challenges of control issues to find balance and fulfillment. Take, for instance, Claire, a high-powered executive in a tech company. Claire spent countless hours micromanaging her team, believing that her meticulous oversight was the only way to succeed. The result? Burnout and strained relationships at work and home. Claire decided enough was enough. She began practicing mindfulness, dedicating a few minutes each morning to meditation. This simple practice helped her stay present and reduce anxiety. Claire also sought therapy, where she learned to trust her team and delegate tasks effectively. Over time, she discovered that letting go of control improved her mental health and boosted her team's productivity and creativity.

Then there's Tenisha, a mother of three who struggled with the pressure to be the perfect parent. Tenisha needed to control every aspect of her children's lives, from homework to extracurricular activities. This constant oversight led to tension and resistance from her kids, who felt stifled. Tenisha realized that her need for control was rooted in anxiety and perfectionism. She started attending a local support group for parents, where she found comfort and practical advice from others facing similar struggles. Tenisha learned to foster independence in her children by giving them more responsibilities and trusting them to make their own decisions. The change was remarkable—her children flourished, becoming more self-reliant and confident, while Tenisha felt a weight lifted off her shoulders.

Another inspiring story is that of Melissa, who balanced a demanding career in finance with her role as a single mother. Melissa's perfectionism drove her to control every detail at work and home, leading to relentless stress. She felt societal and cultural pressures to excel in both arenas, which only heightened her anxiety. Melissa decided to take control of her well-being. She started with self-reflection, journaling her thoughts and feelings to understand her triggers. Through this process, she identified that her fear of failure was a significant driver of her control behaviors. Melissa joined a mindfulness course and began practicing yoga, which helped her find inner peace. She also set realistic goals and boundaries, allowing herself to accept that it's okay not to be perfect. Her newfound balance improved her relationships with colleagues and her child, and she found joy in the present moment.

These stories offer valuable insights and strategies to apply to your life. Persistence and resilience are crucial. Change doesn't happen overnight, but small, consistent steps can lead to significant improvements. Self-compassion is equally important. Be kind to yourself, acknowledging that it's okay to have flaws and make mistakes. Accepting yourself as you are is a powerful step towards reducing control behaviors and finding balance. Seeking support from therapy or community groups can provide the encouragement and tools needed to navigate this journey. Remember, you are not alone, and these stories are a testament to the possibility of transformation.

Strategies for Long-Term Change

Sustainable, long-term change is crucial for truly reducing control behaviors. Short-term fixes might provide temporary relief, but lasting change is what brings about real transformation. Long-term change benefits your mental health and relationships by creating a stable foundation. You'll notice reduced anxiety and stress, more balanced interactions, and overall well-being. Relationships flourish when you're not constantly trying to manage every detail. However, maintaining change over time poses challenges. It's easy to fall back into old habits, especially when life gets stressful. Consistency and patience are your allies in this journey.

To create and maintain long-term change, set realistic and achievable goals. Break down your larger objectives into smaller, manageable steps. For instance, if you want to delegate more at work, begin with a single task. Gradually expand as you become more comfortable. Monitoring your progress is equally important. Keep a journal or use an app to track your achievements and setbacks. This helps you see patterns and adjust strategies as needed. For example, if you notice that you tend to micromanage when stressed, you can implement stress-reduction techniques during those times.

Consistency is key to achieving long-term change. Building habits through repetition helps solidify new behaviors. New habits take time to become second nature, so be patient with yourself. Celebrate small wins along the way. Whether it's a successful week of delegating or a day where you managed to stay calm despite the chaos, acknowledge these victories. They build momentum and reinforce positive change.

Consider the story of Anna, a marketing executive who struggled with work-life balance. She set realistic goals to leave the office by 6 PM at least three days a week. Anna tracked her progress in a journal and made adjustments when she noticed patterns of late nights. Over time, she successfully maintained a healthier work-life balance, feeling more present both at work and home. Her relationships improved as she was less stressed and more engaged with her family.

Another example is Donna, a mother who aimed to create a supportive home environment. She introduced small changes, like weekly family meetings, to discuss everyone's needs and feelings. Donna consistently applied these changes, monitoring their impact on family dynamics. Celebrating small wins, like her children opening up more during these meetings, motivated her to keep going. Over time, these practices became ingrained in their family routine, fostering a more supportive and understanding home environment.

Consistency and patience are essential. It's about making gradual changes that stick. By setting realistic goals, monitoring progress, and celebrating small victories, you can achieve long-term change that significantly reduces control behaviors and enhances your quality of life.

In the next chapter, we'll explore how to build a support network to enhance your well-being further.

TEN

Building a Support Network

Picture yourself sitting in a cozy coffee shop, sipping your latte, and suddenly, you feel the world's weight lifting off your shoulders. Across the table, your best friend listens intently, offering comfort and wisdom. In these moments, you realize the profound impact a strong support network can have on your mental well-being. No one can navigate life's challenges alone, and having a reliable support system can make all the difference.

Importance of a Support Network

A strong support network is like a safety net, catching you when you stumble and lifting you when you're down. The value of having a close-knit circle of friends, family, and professional support cannot be overstated, especially when managing control behaviors and maintaining mental health. Friends provide a listening ear and a different perspective, helping you see situations from angles you may not have considered. They can offer advice grounded in their own experiences, making you feel less isolated in your struggles.

On the other hand, family often provides a sense of unconditional love and acceptance. They know your history, your quirks, and the reasons behind some of your control behaviors. This deep understanding can be comforting, as family members can offer support uniquely tailored to your needs. They can help with practical tasks, provide a shoulder to cry on, or simply be there for a quiet evening at home. However, it's essential to communicate openly with family members about your needs and boundaries to ensure that their support is effective and doesn't inadvertently contribute to your control tendencies.

Professional support, including therapists, counselors, and coaches, is crucial in managing control behaviors. These professionals offer a safe space to explore the root causes of your need for control and develop strategies to address them. Therapists can help you work through past traumas and cognitive distortions that fuel your control issues using evidence-based techniques like Cognitive-Behavioral Therapy (CBT). Coaches, meanwhile, can assist you in setting realistic goals and developing actionable plans to achieve them, providing accountability and motivation along the way.

It's important to recognize that different types of support serve different purposes. Friends and family offer emotional and practical support, while professionals provide specialized guidance and therapeutic interventions. Each type of support complements the others, creating a comprehensive network that addresses various aspects of your well-being.

Having a diverse support network also means you're not overly reliant on one person or type of support. This diversity can prevent burnout and ensure you have multiple sources of strength to draw. For example, while a friend might be great for a late-night chat, a therapist can offer structured interventions to tackle deep-seated issues. Similarly, family members might provide practical help with daily tasks, freeing up your mental space to focus on personal growth and self-care.

It's also worth noting that building and maintaining a support network requires effort and reciprocity. Investing time and energy into your relationships and showing up for others as you'd like them to show up for you is essential. This reciprocity fosters trust and deepens connections, making your support network even more robust. Consider contacting friends regularly, checking in with family members, and attending therapy sessions consistently. These small acts of connection can significantly impact your overall well-being.

Reflecting on your current support network, you might find areas where it could be strengthened. Are there friends you've lost touch with who you could reconnect with? Are there family members you could communicate more openly with? Is there a professional you've been considering seeing but haven't yet taken the step to contact? Taking proactive steps to build and nurture your support network can enhance your ability to manage control behaviors and improve your mental health.

Reflection Exercise: Assessing Your Support Network

Take a moment to reflect on your current support network. Consider the following questions and jot down your thoughts in a journal:

1. Who are the key people in your support network (friends, family, professionals)?
2. How often do you reach out to them for support?
3. Are there areas where your support network could be strengthened?
4. What steps can you take to build or enhance your support network?

By thoughtfully assessing your support network and taking proactive steps to strengthen it, you can create a more resilient foundation for managing control behaviors and maintaining mental health. Remember, you're not alone in this journey; having a strong support network can make all the difference.

Finding and Cultivating Support

Building a support network can feel daunting, especially if you're already juggling numerous responsibilities. But finding like-minded communities and professional help can be incredibly rewarding. Start by considering your interests and current social circles. Are there people you already know who share similar goals or challenges? Reaching out to friends or acquaintances with whom you feel connected can be a great first step. Let them know you're looking to build a supportive network and see if they want to join it. Opening up to others can sometimes pave the way to deeper, more meaningful connections.

Local community groups are another excellent resource. Libraries, community centers, and local bulletin boards list various clubs and groups. Whether it's a book club, a fitness class, or a hobby group, participating in these activities can help you meet people with shared interests. Don't be afraid to attend a meeting to see if it's a good fit. These settings often provide a relaxed atmosphere where you can gradually build relationships without the pressure to open up about personal struggles immediately.

Online communities have become an invaluable support resource for those with busy schedules or limited local options. Websites like Meetup.com offer virtual groups tailored to various interests and needs. From parenting forums to professional development networks, there's likely an online community that aligns with your interests. Social media platforms can also be useful if navigated mindfully. For instance, Facebook groups host various supportive communities where members share advice, experiences, and encouragement. Just ensure you choose positive and constructive groups, avoiding those that might contribute to stress or negativity.

Support groups, both online and offline, provide a structured environment for sharing and listening. Professionals or experienced volunteers often facilitate these groups, ensuring that discussions remain focused and supportive. Look for groups that address specific issues you're dealing with, such as anxiety, parenting, or work-life balance. Participating in a support group can help you realize that you're not alone in your struggles, and hearing others' experiences can offer new perspectives and coping strategies.

Therapy is another cornerstone of a strong support network. A good therapist can offer personalized guidance and help you navigate complex emotions and behaviors. If you're new to therapy, consider asking friends or your primary care doctor for recommendations. Many therapists offer initial consultations, allowing you to find someone you feel comfortable with. Don't be discouraged if it takes a few tries to find the right fit—trust and rapport are crucial for effective therapy.

Coaching can also be incredibly beneficial, especially if you want to achieve specific goals or make significant changes in your life. Life, career, and wellness coaches can provide targeted support and accountability. They can help you break down your goals into manageable steps and offer strategies to overcome obstacles. While coaching is often more action-oriented than therapy, it can complement therapeutic work by providing practical tools and motivation.

If you're a parent, finding and cultivating support can be challenging and incredibly rewarding. Parenting groups, whether in-person or virtual, can offer a sense of camaraderie and shared experience. These groups provide a space to share tips, vent frustrations, and celebrate victories. Look for groups that align with your parenting style and values, ensuring that the advice and support you receive are relevant and helpful.

For professional women, networking groups and associations can be invaluable. Organizations like Lean In Circles, professional guilds, and industry-specific groups offer both support and opportunities for growth. These groups often host events, webinars, and forums where you can connect with peers, mentors, and potential collaborators. Building relationships in these settings can provide emotional support, professional opportunities, and resources.

When cultivating your support network, being proactive and intentional is essential. Regularly contact your contacts, schedule meetups or calls, and participate actively in group activities. Show genuine interest in others' lives and offer support in return. Building a support network is a reciprocal process, and the effort you put in will often be reflected in the support you receive.

Maintaining Healthy Relationships

Imagine you're catching up with a close friend over lunch, and as you both share updates about your lives, you realize how much you rely on each other for support. This kind of relationship doesn't happen overnight; it requires effort, care, and reciprocity. Nurturing and maintaining healthy relationships within your support network is crucial for lasting emotional well-being and mutual growth.

One of the most important aspects of maintaining healthy relationships is the concept of reciprocity. It's not just about what you can get from the relationship but also what you can give. Mutual support is the foundation of any strong relationship. When your friend is going through a tough time, offer a listening ear or a helping hand. Likewise, don't hesitate to lean on them when you need support. This balance of give and take creates a sense of trust and reliability, making both parties feel valued and understood.

Communication is another cornerstone of healthy relationships. It's essential to be open and honest about your needs and boundaries. If you're feeling overwhelmed, let your friend or family member know. They can't read your mind, and clear communication helps avoid misunderstandings. On the flip side, make an effort to listen actively when they share their thoughts and feelings. Active listening means being fully present in the conversation, showing empathy, and reflecting on what you've heard to ensure understanding. This practice strengthens your bond and makes the other person feel heard and valued.

Consistency is key to maintaining healthy relationships. Regular check-ins, whether through text, phone calls, or in-person meetups, help keep the connection strong. It shows that you care and are invested in the relationship. Even a quick message to ask how someone's day is going can make a significant difference. Consistency also means being reliable—following through on promises and being there when you say you will. This reliability builds trust, which is the bedrock of any healthy relationship.

It's also important to practice empathy and understanding. Everyone has their struggles and challenges, and sometimes, your friends or family members might not be able to offer support in the way you need. Instead of feeling hurt or frustrated, try to understand their perspective. Empathy allows you to see things from their point of view, which can deepen your connection and foster a more supportive relationship. Remember, it's not always about having the right words; sometimes, just being there is enough.

Boundaries are crucial in any relationship. They ensure that both parties feel respected and valued. Be clear about your boundaries and respect those of others. If you need alone time to recharge, communicate that openly. Likewise, if a friend sets a boundary, honor it without taking it personally. Boundaries help maintain a healthy balance and prevent feelings of resentment or burnout.

Building rituals can also help maintain healthy relationships. These can be as simple as a weekly coffee date, a monthly book club, or a yearly getaway. Rituals create shared experiences that strengthen your bond and provide something to look forward to. They offer a sense of stability and continuity, which can be comforting amidst life's uncertainties.

Conflict is inevitable in any relationship, but how you handle it can make all the difference. Approach conflicts with a mindset of resolution rather than blame. Use "I" statements to express your feelings without accusing others. For example, say, "I feel hurt when you don't respond to my messages," rather than, "You never respond to me." This approach fosters open dialogue and helps resolve issues without damaging the relationship.

Lastly, celebrate each other's successes and milestones. Whether it's a job promotion, a personal achievement, or a small victory, acknowledging and celebrating these moments shows that you care about their happiness and well-being. It adds a positive dimension to your relationship and creates joyful memories.

Maintaining healthy relationships within your support network requires effort, but the rewards are immense. These relationships provide a sense of belonging, reduce stress, and enhance overall quality of life. By focusing on reciprocity, communication, consistency, empathy, boundaries, rituals, conflict resolution, and celebration, you can nurture relationships that are not only supportive but also deeply fulfilling.

Success Stories

Consider Sarah, a high-achieving marketing executive who always felt like she was carrying the world's weight on her shoulders. Her need to control every aspect of her work and home life left her exhausted and isolated. One day, Sarah decided she couldn't continue like this. She started small by reaching out to a colleague she trusted and respected. Over coffee, she opened up about her struggles with control and anxiety. To her surprise, her colleague shared similar experiences. They began to meet regularly, forming a mini-support network within their office. This simple act of sharing not only eased Sarah's stress but also fostered a sense of camaraderie and mutual support. As Sarah's network grew, she became more willing to delegate tasks and trust her team, leading to increased productivity and a healthier work-life balance.

Then there's Shelly, a single mom navigating the challenges of raising two teenagers while managing a demanding career. Shelly always felt like she had to do it all—be the perfect mom, the ideal employee, and still find time for herself. The constant juggling act took a toll on her mental health, and she knew she needed help. Shelly joined an online parenting group where she found other single moms facing similar challenges. The group became a lifeline, offering practical advice, emotional support, and a safe space to vent. This network taught Shelly to set realistic expectations for herself and her kids. She realized that asking for help wasn't a sign of weakness but a strength. Her support network helped her manage her stress and enriched her parenting experience, making her feel more connected and less alone.

Emma's story highlights the importance of professional support. Emma was a successful lawyer who struggled with perfectionism and control issues. The pressure to be flawless in her career was overwhelming. She decided to seek therapy to understand the root causes of her behavior. Her therapist helped her uncover deep-seated fears of failure and inadequacy that drove her need for control. Through therapy, Emma learned coping strategies to manage her anxiety and perfectionism. Additionally, she joined a professional women's network where she met mentors who provided guidance and support. This combination of professional help and peer support allowed Emma to find balance in her life, reducing her stress and improving her performance at work.

Emma's experience underscores the power of community. As a new mom, Emma felt isolated and overwhelmed by the demands of caring for her newborn. She joined a local mom's group, hoping to find support and advice. What she found was so much more. The group offered a space where she could share her fears, frustrations, and joys without judgment. She formed close friendships with other moms who understood exactly what she was going through. These women became her support network, offering practical help like babysitting swaps and moral support during those sleepless nights. With their help, Emma learned to let go of her need for control and embrace the messiness of motherhood. Her mental health improved, and she felt more confident and capable as a parent.

Consider Charlotte's journey as a professional woman striving to balance her career and personal life. Charlotte was always in control at work, but this often left her feeling drained and disconnected from her loved ones. She joined a professional women's group focused on work-life balance. Through this group, Charlotte met women who were facing similar challenges. They shared strategies for setting boundaries, delegating tasks, and prioritizing self-care. This support network became a source of inspiration and motivation for Charlotte. She learned to set realistic goals for herself, both professionally and personally. Her newfound balance improved her mental health and enhanced her relationships with her family and colleagues.

These success stories illustrate the transformative power of a strong support network. Whether it's friends, family, professional help, or community groups, having a network of supportive individuals can make a significant difference in managing control behaviors and maintaining mental health. As you reflect on these stories, consider the steps you can take to build and nurture your support network.

Remember, you're not alone; seeking support is a courageous and empowering choice.

In the next chapter, we'll explore the importance of embracing flexibility and adaptability in various aspects of life and provide practical tools to help you gracefully navigate unexpected changes and challenges.

ELEVEN

Embracing Flexibility and Adaptability

Imagine you're at a company meeting, the kind that usually makes you tense. The agenda is packed, your to-do list is overflowing, and you've meticulously planned your day to the minute. Suddenly, your boss announces a major shift in the project's direction. Your heart races, your palms sweat, and you feel panicked. What now? This scenario is all too familiar for many of us who crave control. The unexpected throws us off balance, leaving us scrambling to regain a sense of order. But what if I told you that embracing flexibility could help you navigate these changes gracefully, reduce stress, and improve your relationships?

Understanding Flexibility

Flexibility and adaptability are more than just buzzwords; they are essential life skills that can significantly enhance your well-being and effectiveness. Flexibility means adjusting your thoughts, behaviors, and plans in response to new information or changing circumstances. It's about letting go of rigid expectations and finding alternative ways to achieve your goals. Adaptability, on the other hand, is the capacity to thrive in different environments and situations. It involves a willingness to learn, unlearn, and relearn, as well as the ability to cope with uncertainty and change.

In practical terms, flexibility is like adjusting your work schedule to accommodate a sudden family obligation or changing your approach to a project when new challenges arise. Adaptability could involve learning new skills to stay relevant in a rapidly evolving job market or finding joy in unplanned moments of spontaneity. Both qualities require a mindset shift from a fixed to a growth-oriented perspective, where setbacks are seen as opportunities for learning and growth rather than failures.

The benefits of flexibility are manifold. For one, it significantly reduces control tendencies. When you're flexible, you're less likely to feel the need to micromanage every detail of your life. Instead, you can trust that things will work out, even if they don't go as planned. This trust can lead to a profound reduction in anxiety and stress. You'll find yourself more resilient and better able to handle life's ups and downs without feeling overwhelmed.

Flexibility also enhances your relationships. When you're adaptable, you're more open to others' ideas and perspectives. This openness fosters better communication and collaboration, whether at home or work. For instance, if your partner suggests a last-minute change in weekend plans, your ability to adapt can turn a potential conflict into an opportunity for a new adventure. In the workplace, being flexible can make you a more valuable team member, as you'll be better equipped to handle changes in project scope or deadlines with a positive attitude.

Moreover, being flexible can improve your overall well-being. Studies have shown that individuals who exhibit higher levels of flexibility tend to experience greater life satisfaction and emotional stability.

This is because flexibility allows you to navigate life's challenges more effectively, reducing the emotional toll of unexpected events. You become more adept at managing stress, leading to better physical health. Adaptability can also enhance your problem-solving skills, as you'll be more willing to explore different solutions than a single, rigid approach.

Flexibility and adaptability are not innate traits but skills that can be developed with practice. Start by embracing small changes in your daily routine. For example, take a different route to work or try a new hobby. These seemingly minor adjustments can help you become more comfortable with change and uncertainty. Gradually, you can tackle larger shifts, such as taking on a new role at work or moving to a new city. The key is approaching these changes with an open mind and a willingness to learn.

One way to cultivate flexibility is through mindfulness practices. Mindfulness helps you stay present in the moment, reducing the tendency to overthink and stress about the future. When you're mindful, you can approach change with curiosity rather than fear. Mindfulness techniques, such as deep breathing or meditation, can also help you stay calm and focused during turbulent times, making it easier to adapt to new circumstances.

Another effective strategy is to reframe your mindset. Instead of viewing change as a threat, see it as an opportunity for growth. This shift in perspective can significantly change how you respond to new situations. For instance, if a project at work suddenly takes a different direction, view it as a chance to develop new skills or showcase your creativity. This positive outlook can reduce the stress associated with change and make you more resilient.

Building a support network is also crucial for developing flexibility. Surround yourself with people who encourage and support your growth. Whether it's friends, family, or colleagues, having a strong support system can provide the emotional resilience needed to navigate change. They can offer different perspectives and practical advice, making it easier to adapt to new situations.

Remember, flexibility is a journey, not a destination. It's about progress, not perfection. The more you practice, the more natural it will become. Over time, you'll find that flexibility helps you manage control tendencies and enriches your life in ways you never imagined. So, the next time you face an unexpected change, take a deep breath, embrace the uncertainty, and remember that flexibility is your ally in this ever-changing world.

Reflection Exercise: Embracing Flexibility

Take a few moments to reflect on recent changes or challenges in your life. How did you respond to them? Were there opportunities where you could have been more flexible? Name three specific instances where embracing flexibility could have made a positive difference. Consider how you can approach similar situations in the future with a more adaptable mindset. Reflecting on these experiences can help you identify areas for growth and reinforce the importance of flexibility in your daily life.

Developing Adaptability Skills

You're in a busy workday, your schedule packed with meetings and deadlines. Suddenly, your boss drops a new, urgent project on your desk. Your initial reaction is to panic. But instead of letting that stress take over, imagine being able to adapt seamlessly to this change, shifting your priorities without losing your cool. Developing adaptability is key to managing these unexpected challenges without resorting to control. Let's explore some exercises and strategies that can help you become more adaptable in your daily life.

One effective way to develop adaptability is to start small. Begin with minor changes in your routine that don't carry much risk. For example, try switching up your morning routine. If you usually start your day by checking emails, spend the first 30 minutes on a mindfulness exercise or light stretching instead. This small shift can help you become more comfortable with change and break the habit of rigid routines. Over time, these small adaptations can build confidence in handling larger, more significant changes.

Another powerful exercise is to deliberately put yourself in new and unfamiliar situations. This could be as simple as taking a different route to work or trying a new hobby. Exposing yourself to new experiences teaches you to navigate uncertainty and become more comfortable with the unknown. For instance, if you've always been interested in painting but never tried it, sign up for a beginner's class. Learning something new, making mistakes, and improving over time can be incredibly empowering and enhance your ability to adapt to new challenges in other areas of your life.

Practicing mindfulness can also be a game-changer. Mindfulness helps you stay present and focused, reducing the tendency to overthink and stress about future uncertainties. When you practice mindfulness, you learn to observe your thoughts and feelings without judgment, allowing you to respond to changes more calmly and thoughtfully. Try incorporating short mindfulness sessions into your daily routine. Even five minutes of focused breathing or a quick body scan can make a difference. Over time, mindfulness can help you develop a more adaptable mindset, making it easier to go with the flow when unexpected changes arise.

Adopting a growth mindset is another crucial strategy. A growth mindset, instead of a fixed mindset, embraces challenges as opportunities for learning and growth. When you encounter an unexpected change, instead of seeing it as a threat, view it as a chance to develop new skills or gain new insights. For example, if a project at work takes an unexpected turn, see it as an opportunity to showcase your problem-solving skills or learn a new aspect of the business. This shift in perspective can reduce the stress associated with change and make you more resilient.

Building a support network is also essential for developing adaptability. Surround yourself with people who encourage and support your growth. Whether it's friends, family, or colleagues, having a strong support system can provide the emotional resilience needed to navigate change. They can offer different perspectives and practical advice, making it easier to adapt to new situations. For instance, discussing a significant change at work with a trusted colleague can provide valuable insights and help you feel more confident handling it.

To handle unexpected changes without resorting to control, it's important to develop a flexible mindset. This involves being open to new possibilities and adjusting your plans as needed. One way to cultivate this mindset is to practice saying "yes" more often. When opportunities arise, even outside your comfort zone, consider saying yes and seeing where it leads. This doesn't mean you should agree to everything, but being more open to new experiences can help you become more adaptable.

Another strategy is to create contingency plans. While predicting every possible outcome is impossible, having a few backup plans can make it easier to adapt when things don't go as expected. For example, if you're planning a big presentation at work, think about potential obstacles that could arise, such as technical issues or unexpected questions. Having a plan in place for these scenarios can reduce anxiety and help you feel more prepared to handle whatever comes your way.

It's also helpful to practice letting go of the need for perfection. Understand that things won't always go according to plan, and that's okay. Instead of striving for perfection, focus on progress and learning. For instance, if a project doesn't turn out exactly as you envisioned, take a step back and evaluate what you've learned from the experience. This can help you see the value in the process itself rather than just the outcome.

Journaling can be a valuable tool for developing adaptability. Take time each day to reflect on how you handled unexpected changes or challenges. Write down what went well, what didn't, and what you can learn from the experience. This practice can help you identify patterns in your behavior and develop strategies for responding more adaptively in the future.

Lastly, practice gratitude. Focusing on what you're grateful for makes it easier to maintain a positive outlook even when things don't go as planned. Try keeping a gratitude journal where you write down three things you're grateful for daily. This simple practice can shift your mindset from scarcity and control to abundance and adaptability.

Developing adaptability is a continuous process, but with practice, it can become second nature. By incorporating these exercises and strategies into your daily life, you can become more resilient, reduce your need for control, and easily navigate life's unexpected challenges.

Real-Life Application

Meet Val, a marketing executive who used to feel like she had to control every aspect of her job and home life. Val was known for her meticulous planning and ability to juggle multiple tasks. However, this constant need for control started taking a toll on her mental health and her relationships. She felt perpetually stressed and anxious, and her colleagues often felt micromanaged.

Val decided it was time to make a change. She started by incorporating small changes into her daily routine. Instead of sticking to her rigid schedule, she allowed herself some flexibility. If a meeting ran over time, she didn't panic. She simply adjusted her plan for the day. This small shift in mindset made a huge difference. She felt more relaxed and was able to focus better on her tasks.

In her personal life, Val applied the same principles. She started saying "yes" to spontaneous plans with friends and family. Instead of planning every detail of her weekends, she left room for unplanned activities. This made her weekends more enjoyable and less stressful. Val's relationships improved as her friends and family appreciated her newfound spontaneity and openness.

Another inspiring story is Jasmine, a single mother of two who works as a nurse. Jasmine's job is demanding, with long shifts and the occasional emergency call. She used to feel overwhelmed by the unpredictability of her schedule and the demands of parenting. Jasmine decided to embrace flexibility to manage her stress better. She began by creating a more adaptable daily routine. She arranged for a neighbor to pick up her kids from school if she had to stay late at work. She also learned to let go of the need for a spotless home, focusing instead on spending quality time with her children.

Jasmine also practiced mindfulness to stay present and reduce anxiety. She would take a few minutes each morning to meditate and set positive intentions for the day. This practice helped her stay calm and focused, even when her day didn't go as planned. Jasmine's new approach improved her mental health and strengthened her bond with her children. They appreciated her relaxed demeanor and the time they spent together, free from the stress of a rigid schedule.

Then there's Kim, a project manager in a tech company. Kim's role required her to oversee multiple projects simultaneously, each with its challenges and deadlines. She often found herself trying to control every detail, which led to burnout and strained relationships with her team. Kim took a different approach by delegating tasks and trusting her team more. She started by identifying tasks that others could handle and trained her team to take on more responsibilities. This lightened her workload and empowered her team members, making them feel more valued and engaged.

Kim also worked on her adaptability by embracing a growth mindset. She viewed a project as an opportunity to learn and grow whenever it faced unexpected changes. Instead of stressing over deviations from the plan, she focused on finding creative solutions. This positive attitude was contagious, and her team became more resilient and innovative. Kim's flexibility and adaptability improved her work-life balance and made her a more effective leader.

Alison's story is another great example. She is a freelance graphic designer who used to struggle with the unpredictability of freelancing. The feast-or-famine cycle of freelance work often left her feeling anxious and stressed. Alison decided to embrace flexibility by diversifying her client base and income streams. She started offering online workshops and selling digital products in addition to her client work. This provided a more stable income and allowed her to explore new creative avenues.

Alison also practiced flexibility in her daily routine. Instead of sticking to a strict 9-to-5 schedule, she allowed herself to work during her most productive hours, whether early in the morning or late at night. She also made time for self-care activities like yoga and reading, which helped her stay balanced and energized. Alison's adaptable approach to freelancing reduced her stress and made her work more enjoyable and fulfilling.

These real-life stories demonstrate the power of embracing flexibility and adaptability. Whether it's adjusting your daily routine, delegating tasks, or exploring new opportunities, being flexible can significantly reduce stress and improve your overall well-being. It can also enhance your relationships, making you more open to others' ideas and perspectives. By learning to go with the flow, you can navigate life's challenges more easily and confidently.

As we've seen, flexibility is not just about reacting to changes but proactively creating a life that allows adaptation. It's about finding balance and embracing the unexpected moments that make life rich and fulfilling. In the next chapter, we'll explore how to create a personal action plan to apply these principles in your own life.

TWELVE

Creating a Personal Action Plan

See yourself sitting at your favorite café, savoring a cup of coffee, and feeling a bit overwhelmed by the sheer number of things on your to-do list. You've read about mindfulness, deep breathing exercises, and the importance of setting boundaries, but putting it all into practice feels daunting. That's where a personal action plan comes in. It's your roadmap to reducing control behaviors and achieving a balanced, fulfilling life. You can make meaningful progress without feeling overwhelmed by breaking down your goals into manageable steps.

Developing an Action Plan

Creating a personalized action plan starts with understanding your unique needs and challenges. Think of it as crafting a tailored recipe for success that considers your specific ingredients and desired outcomes. Start by identifying the areas where you struggle most with control. Is it at work where you find yourself micromanaging every detail? Or at home, where you feel the need to oversee every aspect of your family's routine? Once you've pinpointed these areas, you can begin setting clear, achievable goals.

Begin by setting SMART goals—Specific, Measurable, Achievable, Relevant, and Time-bound goals. For example, instead of saying, "I want to stop micromanaging at work," you might set a goal like, "I will delegate at least one task to a team member each day for the next month." This goal is specific (delegating tasks), measurable (one task per day), achievable (manageable within your daily routine), relevant (directly addresses micromanaging), and time-bound (over the next month).

Next, break these goals down into smaller, actionable steps. Let's take the goal of delegating tasks at work. The first step might be to identify tasks that can be delegated. Make a list of all your current responsibilities and highlight those that don't require your direct involvement. The next step could be communicating with your team, explaining the importance of delegation and how it will benefit you and them. Finally, you might set a reminder to delegate one task each day, gradually building this new habit.

Tracking your progress as you work on these steps is crucial. Keeping a journal or using a digital tracker can be incredibly helpful. Note each task you delegate and reflect on how it feels to let go of control. Are you experiencing less stress? How is your team responding? Tracking these details will help you see the progress you're making and stay motivated.

In addition to tracking progress, reflection is a key component of your action plan. Set aside time each week to review your journal or tracker. Reflect on what's working well and what challenges you've faced. This reflection period allows you to celebrate your successes and identify areas where you might need to adjust your approach. For example, if you find that delegating tasks has reduced your stress but still feel overwhelmed by your workload, you might need to set additional boundaries or seek further support.

To help you get started, I've included a template for setting goals, tracking progress, and reflecting on achievements. Feel free to customize it to fit your needs.

Personal Action Plan Template

Goal Setting:

1. **Identify Areas of Struggle:**
    - Work: Micromanaging tasks
    - Home: Overseeing family routines
    - Relationships: Controlling conversations
2. **Set SMART Goals:**
    - Work: "I will delegate at least one task to a team member each day for the next month."
    - Home: "I will allow my partner to handle dinner plans twice a week."
    - Relationships: "I will practice active listening without interrupting during conversations."

Actionable Steps:

1. **Break Down Goals:**
    - Delegating Tasks at Work:
        - List all current responsibilities
        - Highlight tasks that can be delegated
        - Communicate with the team about delegation
        - Set daily reminders to delegate one task
2. **Home and Relationships:**
    - Allow Partner to Handle Dinner Plans:
        - Discuss the plan with your partner
        - Schedule which days they'll handle dinner
        - Provide support without taking over
    - Practice Active Listening:

- Set a goal to listen during one conversation each day actively
- Reflect on the experience in your journal

Tracking Progress:

1. **Daily Tracking:**
    - Use a journal or digital tracker to note each task you delegate, each dinner plan handled by your partner, and each time you practice active listening.
    - Record your feelings and observations.
2. **Weekly Reflection:**
    - Review your journal or tracker.
    - Reflect on what's working well and any challenges faced.
    - Adjust your approach as needed.

Reflection Questions:

1. **Successes:**
    - What tasks did I successfully delegate this week?
    - How did it feel to let go of control?
    - What positive changes have I noticed in my stress levels and team dynamics?
2. **Challenges:**
    - What obstacles did I encounter?
    - How can I address these challenges moving forward?
    - Do I need to adjust my goals or steps?
3. **Adjustments:**
    - Are there additional boundaries I need to set?
    - Is there further support I need to seek?
    - How can I continue to build on my successes?

Creating a personal action plan isn't about achieving perfection; it's about making steady progress toward a more balanced and fulfilling life. Be kind to yourself throughout this process. Remember that change takes time and effort, and it's okay to make adjustments along the way. Celebrate your successes, no matter how small, and use any setbacks as learning opportunities.

Having a support system in place is also helpful as you work on your action plan. Share your goals with a trusted friend, family member, or mentor who can offer encouragement and hold you accountable. Having someone to check in with can make a significant difference in staying motivated and committed to your plan.

Incorporate self-care practices into your action plan to support your overall well-being. Mindfulness exercises, deep breathing techniques, and regular physical activity can help manage stress and keep you focused. Make sure to schedule time for these activities, treating them as non-negotiable parts of your routine.

Finally, be patient with yourself. Reducing control behaviors and embracing flexibility is a journey that requires persistence and self-compassion. Celebrate each step forward and acknowledge your effort to create positive change. You're taking important steps toward a more balanced, fulfilling life, and that's something to be proud of.

Setting Milestones and Rewards

Imagine you're climbing a mountain. The peak feels impossibly far away, but there are small plateaus along the way where you can rest, catch your breath, and appreciate how far you've come. This is what setting milestones is like on your path to reducing control behaviors. Milestones are essential because they break down a daunting goal into manageable chunks, making progress feel achievable and less overwhelming.

Milestones act as mini-goals that keep you focused and motivated. For example, if your primary goal is to let go of micromanaging at work, a milestone could be delegating one significant task per week. Another milestone might be to receive positive feedback from a team member about your delegation skills. These smaller goals help you maintain momentum and provide opportunities to celebrate your progress, reinforcing your motivation to continue.

Celebrating these milestones is just as crucial as setting them. Think of it as giving yourself a well-deserved pat on the back. Recognition, whether from yourself or others, can significantly boost your morale and reinforce positive behaviors. It's important to choose rewards that are meaningful to you, and that genuinely feel like a treat. These rewards don't have to be extravagant; they just need to be something that brings you joy and satisfaction.

Incorporating rewards can be as simple as allowing yourself some extra downtime. For instance, after successfully delegating tasks for a week, you might reward yourself with a relaxing evening off, indulging in a favorite hobby, or spending time with loved ones. If you've reached a more significant milestone, such as consistently practicing mindfulness for a month, consider treating yourself to a spa day or a weekend getaway. The key is that the reward should feel like a genuine acknowledgment of your hard work and progress.

Another idea for meaningful rewards is to invest in something that further supports your goals. Suppose you've been working on reducing control behaviors at home by allowing your partner to handle more responsibilities. As a reward, you might invest in a family activity that fosters togetherness and fun, like a game night or a day trip. This not only celebrates your progress but also strengthens the bonds within your family.

You can also consider rewards that promote self-care and well-being. For example, after reaching a milestone, treat yourself to a new book, a yoga class, or a session with a coach or therapist. These rewards not only acknowledge your achievements but also contribute to your ongoing personal growth and mental health.

In addition to personal rewards, sharing your milestones and achievements with others can be incredibly powerful. Tell a close friend, family member, or mentor about your progress. Their encouragement and recognition can further boost your confidence and motivation. You might even consider celebrating together, such as going out for a celebratory meal or engaging in a fun activity that you both enjoy.

It's also helpful to document your milestones and rewards. Keeping a visual record, like a progress chart or a journal, can provide a tangible reminder of how far you've come. Each time you look at this record, you'll see a visual representation of your efforts and successes, which can be incredibly motivating during challenging times.

Creating a milestone and reward checklist can be beneficial for those who thrive on structure. Write down your primary goal, break it into smaller milestones, and next to each milestone, note the reward you'll give yourself upon achieving it. This checklist can serve as a roadmap, guiding you through your journey with clear markers of progress and celebration.

As you continue to reach milestones and celebrate your successes, you'll likely notice a shift in your mindset. The process of setting and achieving small goals can build your confidence and reinforce the belief that you are capable of change. It can also help you develop a more positive and proactive attitude toward your goals, making the overall process feel less daunting.

Remember, the purpose of rewards is not just to mark progress but to make the journey enjoyable and fulfilling. By acknowledging your efforts and celebrating your achievements, you're reinforcing the positive changes you're making in your life. This not only helps you stay motivated but also makes the process of reducing control behaviors a rewarding and enriching experience in itself.

In essence, setting milestones and celebrating progress is about creating a balanced and sustainable approach to personal growth. It's about recognizing that each step you take, no matter how small, is a victory worth celebrating. So, as you continue on your path toward reducing control behaviors, make sure to pause, appreciate your progress, and reward yourself for the incredible effort you're putting in.

Maintaining Motivation

Staying motivated on your personal growth journey can be challenging, especially when life throws curveballs your way. But keeping that spark alive is crucial to making lasting changes. One effective way to stay motivated is to regularly remind yourself why you started this journey in the first place. Visualize the benefits of reducing control behaviors—imagine less stress, more fulfilling relationships, and a greater sense of peace. Write down these benefits and place them somewhere visible, like your bathroom mirror or your workspace. This constant reminder of your "why" can reignite your motivation on tough days.

Another key to maintaining motivation is to surround yourself with positive influences. Engage with a community of like-minded individuals who are also working on personal growth. This could be a local support group, an online forum, or even a few close friends who share similar goals. Sharing your experiences, challenges, and successes with others creates a sense of camaraderie and support. Knowing you're not alone in your journey can make all the difference. Plus, celebrating each other's milestones can be incredibly uplifting and encouraging.

It's also helpful to break your goals into smaller, more manageable tasks. When you see progress in smaller increments, it feels less overwhelming and more achievable. Instead of focusing on the end goal, concentrate on the next step you need to take. For example, if your goal is to delegate more at work, start with one small task. Once you've successfully delegated that task, move on to the next. This approach not only makes the process more manageable but also allows you to celebrate small wins along the way, which boosts your motivation.

Creating a routine can also keep you on track. Incorporate time for self-reflection, mindfulness, or any other practices that help you stay focused and calm. Consistency is key. Even on days when you don't feel like it, sticking to your routine can help maintain momentum. Remember, it's okay to have off days. What matters is getting back on track. A routine provides structure, which can be comforting and motivating, especially when life feels chaotic.

Setbacks are inevitable, but they don't have to derail your progress. When you face a setback, it's important to approach it with a growth mindset. Instead of viewing the setback as a failure, see it as a learning opportunity. Ask yourself what you can learn from the experience and how you can apply that lesson moving forward. This shift in perspective can turn setbacks into valuable stepping stones on your path to growth. Remember, progress isn't always linear, and that's okay.

Another effective strategy is to mix things up. Sometimes, monotony can sap your motivation. If you find yourself in a rut, try changing your approach. This could mean switching up your routine, trying a new mindfulness exercise, or setting a new short-term goal. Variety keeps things interesting and can rekindle your enthusiasm. Experiment with different strategies until you find what works best for you.

Accountability is another powerful motivator. Share your goals with someone you trust and ask them to hold you accountable. Regular check-ins with this person can keep you focused and committed. Knowing that someone else is invested in your progress can provide an extra boost of motivation. Whether it's a friend, family member, or coach, having someone to support and encourage you can make a significant difference.

Lastly, practice self-compassion. Be kind to yourself, especially on tough days. Remember that personal growth is a process, not a destination. It's okay to make mistakes and have setbacks. What's important is that you're making an effort and taking steps toward positive change. Treat yourself with the same kindness and understanding that you would offer a friend. This self-compassion not only boosts your motivation but also fosters a healthier, more positive mindset.

In summary, staying motivated involves a combination of reminding yourself of your why, surrounding yourself with positive influences, breaking goals into manageable tasks, creating a routine, viewing setbacks as learning opportunities, mixing things up, seeking accountability, and practicing self-compassion. These strategies can help you stay committed to your action plan and continue making progress toward your goals. Personal growth is a journey, and maintaining motivation is key to navigating it successfully. As you continue on this path, remember to celebrate your progress, no matter how small, and keep pushing forward.

Conclusion

It's been quite a journey, hasn't it? We've dived deep into understanding what it means to be a control freak and, more importantly, how to release that control. This book opened with recognizing and understanding control behaviors, helping you see how they manifest in daily life and their impact on mental health and relationships. We then moved on to practical tools like mindfulness and deep breathing exercises to help you manage stress and anxiety.

We explored enhancing mental health with techniques like Cognitive-Behavioral Therapy (CBT), stress-reduction methods, and the importance of sleep, nutrition, and exercise. We also delved into the power of self-reflection, using journaling and reflective questions to uncover hidden anxieties and triggers. Understanding your past and identifying fear-based thoughts were crucial steps toward building self-awareness.

Then, we focused on improving relationship dynamics through effective communication, building trust, navigating conflicts, and setting healthy boundaries. We also covered balancing professional and personal life with productivity hacks, delegation techniques, and strategies for managing workplace stress. And let's not forget the importance of managing technology and digital distractions.

Parenting without control was another significant topic, emphasizing setting healthy boundaries, encouraging independence, and creating a nurturing home environment. Navigating societal and cultural pressures helped you break free from traditional roles and embrace your authentic self. Building a support network and embracing flexibility and adaptability rounded out our journey, giving you the tools to navigate life's challenges with grace and resilience.

Key Takeaways:

- **Self-Awareness:** Understanding and recognizing control behaviors is the first step toward change.
- **Practical Tools:** Mindfulness, deep-breathing exercises, and CBT can significantly reduce anxiety and stress.
- **Healthy Relationships:** Effective communication, trust-building, and setting boundaries are essential for healthy relationships.
- **Work-Life Balance:** Productivity hacks, delegation, and managing workplace stress can help you balance your professional and personal life.
- **Parental Guidance:** Setting healthy boundaries and encouraging independence in your children fosters a nurturing environment.
- **Societal Pressures:** Breaking free from traditional roles and embracing your authentic self is empowering.
- **Support Networks:** Building and maintaining a support network is crucial for ongoing growth and resilience.
- **Flexibility:** Embracing flexibility and adaptability helps you navigate life's changes with ease.

Now, it's time for a call to action. Take a moment to reflect on what you've learned and how it applies to your life. What small steps can you take today to start releasing control and embracing a more balanced, fulfilling life? Maybe it's delegating a task at work, practicing mindfulness for a few minutes each day, or setting a new boundary in a relationship. Whatever it is, commit to taking that first step.

Remember, change doesn't happen overnight. It's a journey, and every step you take, no matter how small, is progress. Be kind to yourself, celebrate your achievements, and don't be afraid to ask for help when needed. I'm here to support you every step of the way. Whether it's through continued reading, joining a support group, or seeking professional help, know that you're not alone.

In closing, I want to leave you with an empowering note: You have the power to change your life. You can achieve a more balanced, fulfilling life by releasing control, enhancing self-awareness, and nurturing emotional growth. Your relationships will flourish, your mental health will improve, and you'll find a newfound sense of peace and joy. Embrace this journey with an open heart and mind, and remember that every step you take brings you closer to the life you deserve.

Keep going, and never forget that you're stronger and more capable than you realize. The path to a more balanced, fulfilling life is within your reach. You've got this!

References

- The Origins and Future of Control Theory in Psychology https://journals.sagepub.com/doi/10.1037/gpr0000057
- The relationship between self-control and mental ... NCBI
- https://www.ncbi.nlm.nih.gov/pmc/articles/PMC10644003/#:~:text=Self%2Dcontrol%20is%20often%20associated,under%2Dcontrol%20(24)
- Controlling People: 12 Signs to Watch For
- https://www.healthline.com/health/controlling-people
- Controlling Behavior: 7 Signs To Look For https://www.webmd.com/mental-health/signs-controlling-behavior
- 5 mindfulness techniques for letting go of control https://www.fastcompany.com/90424137/5-mindfulness-techniques-for-letting-go-of-control
- Breathing Techniques for Stress Relief https://www.webmd.com/balance/stress-management/stress-relief-breathing-techniques
- 10 Strategies for Better Time Management https://extension.uga.edu/publications/detail.html?number=C1042&title=time-management-10-strategies-for-better-time-management
- 7 Ways to Set Realistic Expectations for Yourself https://psychcentral.com/health/suggestions-for-setting-realistic-expectations-with-yourself
- How Cognitive Behavioral Therapy Can Treat Your Anxiety https://www.healthline.com/health/anxiety/cbt-for-anxiety
- Women and Stress
- https://my.clevelandclinic.org/health/articles/5545-women-and-stress
- Mental Health and Sleep
- https://www.sleepfoundation.org/mental-health
- Nutritional psychiatry: Your brain on food https://www.health.harvard.edu/blog/nutritional-psychiatry-your-brain-on-food-201511168626
- The Power of Journaling for Well-being: A Path to Self ... https://dhwblog.dukehealth.org/the-power-of-journaling-for-well-being-a-path-to-self-discovery-and-healing/#:~:text=It%20offers%20the%20benefits%20of,happier%20and%20more%20balanced%20life
- 87 Self-Reflection Questions for Introspection [+Exercises] https://positivepsychology.com/introspection-self-reflection/
- How to Identify and Manage Your Emotional Triggers https://www.healthline.com/health/mental-health/emotional-triggers

References

- Understanding the Impact of Trauma - NCBI
- https://www.ncbi.nlm.nih.gov/books/NBK207191/
- 7 Keys to Effective Communication Skills in Relationships https://seattlechristiancounseling.com/articles/7-keys-to-effective-communication-skills-in-relationships
- How to Build Trust in a Relationship, According to a Therapist https://www.verywellmind.com/how-to-build-trust-in-a-relationship-5207611
- How Emotion Regulation Can Transform Your Conflict Cycle https://www.gottman.com/blog/emotion-regulation-transform-your-conflict-cycle/
- 7 Active Listening Techniques For Better Communication https://www.verywellmind.com/what-is-active-listening-3024343
- 5 Productivity Apps Every Working Mom Should Know About https://womenlovetech.com/5-productivity-apps-every-working-mom-should-know-about/
- How to Delegate Effectively: 9 Tips for Managers - HBS Online https://online.hbs.edu/blog/post/how-to-delegate-effectively
- Nine Strategies Busy Professionals Can Use To Reduce ... https://www.forbes.com/sites/forbescoachescouncil/2017/08/11/nine-strategies-busy-professionals-can-use-to-reduce-stress/
- 10 Work Life Balance Tips for Women https://www.moneylion.com/learn/10-work-life-balance-tips-for-women/
- Setting Healthy Boundaries for Kids: Why and How to Do It https://calmerry.com/blog/parenting/how-to-set-boundaries-for-children-without-yelling-threats-and-bribes/
- Promoting children's independence: What parents say vs do https://mottpoll.org/reports/promoting-childrens-independence-what-parents-say-vs-do
- Positive Reinforcement for Kids: 11+ Examples for Parents https://positivepsychology.com/parenting-positive-reinforcement/
- Parenting Stress and Self-Care https://getparentingtips.com/parents/health/parenting-stress-and-self-care/
- Understanding Gender Roles and Their Effect On Our ... https://www.verywellmind.com/understanding-gender-roles-and-their-effect-on-our-relationships-7499408
- Challenging Societal Expectations: Stories of Resilient ... https://www.becomebraveenough.com/blog/challenging-societal-expectations-stories-of-resilient-women

References

- Understanding 'Societal Expectations' and Stereotypes
https://www.linkedin.com/pulse/understanding-societal-expectations-stereotypes-kim-jones-zcaxf

Women Breaking Free

Your Voice Matters!

"The most powerful way to inspire change is to share your story and lift others along the way." – Unknown

Hey there!

First of all, thank you for diving into *Women Breaking Free*. I hope it's been as empowering for you as it was for me to write. We've been on this journey together—exploring how to let go of control, overcome perfectionism, and find a sense of peace in a world that often feels overwhelming. Now, I have one small favor to ask.

Imagine this: There's someone out there, just like you. She's overwhelmed, stressed, and trying to do it all, just like you might have been when you first picked up this book. Maybe she's a professional juggling too much, a mom trying to hold it all together, or someone simply looking for a little more peace in her life.

You can be the reason she finds this book, the reason she gets the help she needs to start breaking free. All you need to do is leave a quick review. Your thoughts could be the encouragement she's looking for to take the leap and start her own journey toward peace and balance.

Why Leave a Review?

- It **costs nothing** but helps others find the support they need.
- It can **change someone's life**—maybe even help her reclaim her peace and freedom.
- Your voice helps me **reach more women** who need to hear this message.

It Only Takes 60 Seconds!

Click the link or scan the QR code below to leave your review. It's quick, easy, and it'll help more women discover the tools to live a more peaceful, balanced life.

Your review doesn't have to be fancy. A few sentences sharing how this book has helped you will make a difference. Whether you found a new way to manage stress, learned to set boundaries, or simply felt seen—your experience matters.

Thank you from the bottom of my heart for being part of this journey with me. I'm so grateful for you.

Your biggest fan,

Selene Meadows

P.S. Helping others is one of the most powerful things we can do. If you know someone who might benefit from this book, please pass it along or share the link. We're all in this together!